Hippocrene

CHILDREN'S ILLUSTRATED CZECH DICTIONARY

ENGLISH - CZECH
CZECH - ENGLISH

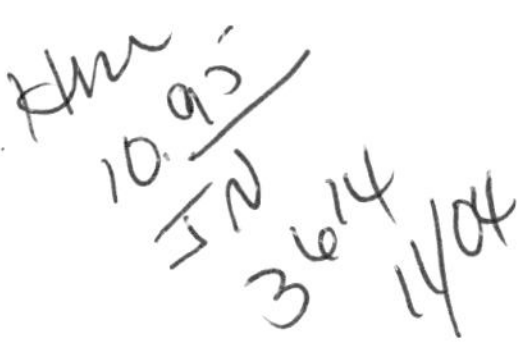

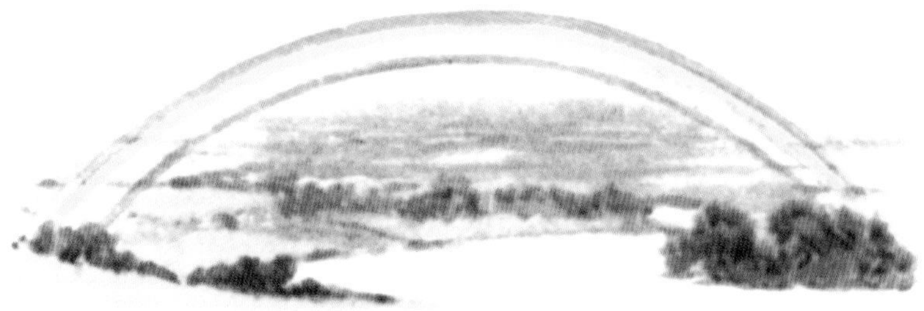

Compiled and translated by the Editors of Hippocrene Books

Interior illustrations by S. Grant (24, 81, 88); J. Gress (page 10, 21, 24, 37, 46, 54, 59, 65, 72, 75, 77); K. Migliorelli (page 13, 14, 18, 19, 20, 21, 22, 25, 31, 32, 37, 39, 40, 46, 47, 66, 71, 75, 76, 82, 86, 87); B. Swidzinska (page 9, 11, 12, 13, 14, 16, 23, 27, 28, 30, 32, 33, 35, 37, 38, 41, 42, 45, 46, 47, 48, 49, 50, 52, 53, 56, 57, 58, 59, 60, 61, 62, 63, 66, 68, 69, 70, 71, 72, 73, 75, 77, 78, 79, 83), N. Zhukov (page 8, 13, 14, 17, 18, 23, 27, 29, 33, 34, 39, 40, 41, 52, 64, 65, 71, 72, 73, 78, 84, 86, 88).

Design, prepress, and production: Graafiset International, Inc.

Cataloging-in-Publication Data available from the Library of Congress.

ISBN 0-7818-0711-5

Printed in Hong Kong.

For information, address:
Hippocrene Books, Inc.
171 Madison Avenue
New York, NY 10016

INTRODUCTION

With their absorbent minds, infinite curiosities and excellent memories, children have enormous capacities to master many languages. All they need is exposure and encouragement.

The easiest way to learn a foreign language is to simulate the same natural method by which a child learns English. The natural technique is built on the concept that language is representational of concrete objects and ideas. The use of pictures and words are the natural way for children to begin to acquire a new language.

The concept of this Illustrated Dictionary is to allow children to build vocabulary and initial competency naturally. Looking at the pictorial content of the Dictionary and saying and matching the words in connection to the drawings gives children the opportunity to discover the foreign language and thus, a new way to communicate.

The drawings in the Dictionary are designed to capture children's imaginations and make the learning process interesting and entertaining, as children return to a word and picture repeatedly until they begin to recognize it.

The beautiful images and clear presentation make this dictionary a wonderful tool for unlocking your child's multilingual potential.

Deborah Dumont, M.A., M.Ed.,
Child Psychologist and Educational Consultant

Czech Pronunciation

b, d, f, k, l, m, n, p, s, t, v, z are all prounounced as in English

The following letters are unique to Czech or pronounced differently than their English counterparts:

Letter	Pronunciation system used
a	**ah** like the *u* in English 'nut' or like the *o* in the English 'come'
á	**aa** like the *a* in English 'father' [long]
c	**ts** like the *ts* in English 'bats'
č	**ch** like the *ch* in English 'church'
d'	**dy** a soft *d*, like the *d* in English 'due'
d'	**d'** soft letter at the end of a word
e	**e** like the *e* in English 'bed'
é	**eh** a long *e*
g	**g** like the *g* in English 'give'
h	**h** like the *h* in English 'him'
ch	**kh** like the *ch* in the pronunciation of Scottish 'loch'
i	**i** like the *ee* in English 'eel' but short
í	**ee** like the *ee* in English 'beetle'
j	**y** like the *y* in English 'you'
n'	**ny** a soft *n*, like the *n* in English 'news'
n'	**n'** soft letter at the end of a word
o	**o** like the *o* in English 'moss'
ó	**oh** a long *o*, like the *oo* in English 'door'
r	**r** a trilled *r*, like the *rr* in English 'burrow'
ř	**rzh** a unique sound to Czech, like *r* and *ž* said together
š	**sh** like the *sh* in English 'sheep'
t'	**ty** a soft *t*, like the *t* in English 'tube'
t'	**t'** soft letter at the end of a word
u	**u** like the *u* in English 'put'
ú/ů	**oo** like the *oo* in English 'pool'
y	**i** like the *i* in English 'sit'
ý	**ee** a long *i*, like the *ee* in English 'beetle'
ž	**zh** like the *s* in English 'treasure'

Dipthongs:

ou	**ow** like the *ow* in English 'slow'
au	**aw** like the *ou* in English 'out'

When followed by an e, the soft consonant is written as dě, ně, or tě accordingly.
The stress is always on the *first* syllable in the Czech language.
Please note that the letters 'r' and 'l' are considered 'semi-vowels' in some Czech words.

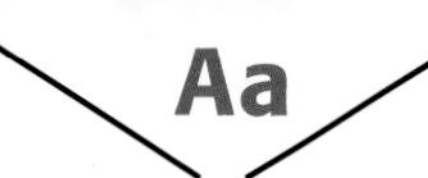

airplane | **(to) letadlo** *(to) le-tahd-lo*

alligator | **(ten) aligátor** *(ten) ah-li-gaa-tor*

alphabet | **(ta) abeceda** *(tah) ah-be-tse-dah*

antelope | **(ta) antilopa** *(tah) ahn-ti-lo-pah*

antlers | **(ty) parohy** *(ti) pah-ro-hi*

apple **(to) jablko**
(to) jah-bl-ko

aquarium **(to) akvárium**
(to) ahk-vaa-ri-yum

arch **(ta) klenba**
(tah) klen-bah

arrow **(ten) šíp**
(ten) sheep

autumn **(ten) podzim**
(ten) pod-zim

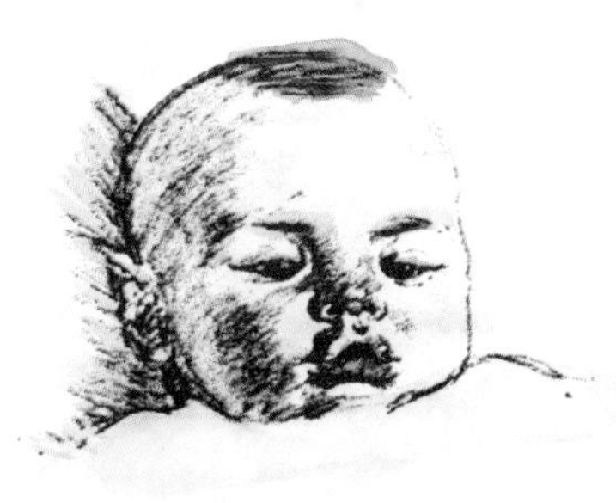

baby **(to) miminko**
(to) mi-min-ko

backpack **(ten) batoh**
(ten) bah-tokh

badger **(ten) jezevec**
(ten) ye-ze-vets

baker **(ten) pekař**
(ten) pe-kahrzh

ball **(ten) míč**
(ten) meech

balloon **(ten) balón**
(ten) bah-lohn

banana (ten) banán
(ten) bah-naan

barley (ten) ječmen
(ten) yech-men

barrel (ten) sud
(ten) sud

basket (ten) košík
(ten) ko-sheek

bat (ten) netopýr
(ten) ne-to-peer

beach (ta) pláž
(tah) plaazh

bear **(ten) medvěd**
(ten) med-vyed

beaver **(ten) bobr**
(ten) bo-br

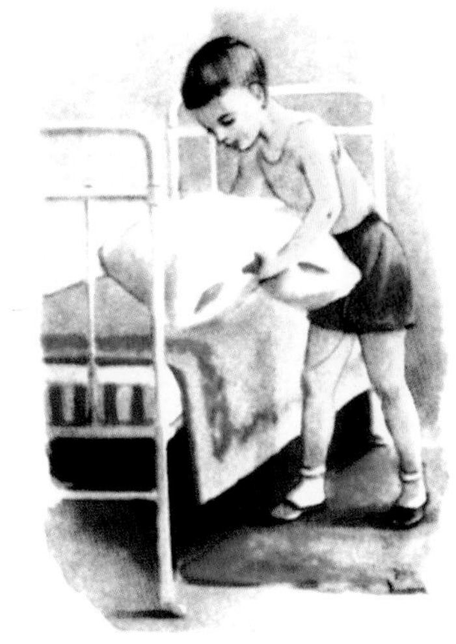

bed **(ta) postel**
(tah) pos-tel

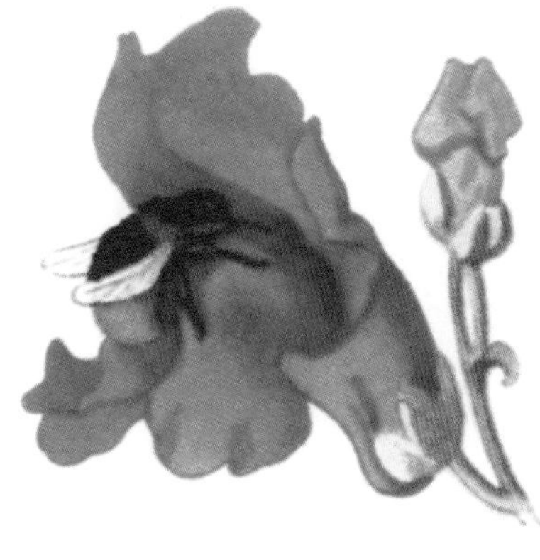

bee **(ta) včela**
(tah) fche-lah

beetle **(ten) brouk**
(ten) browk

bell **(ten) zvon**
(ten) zvon

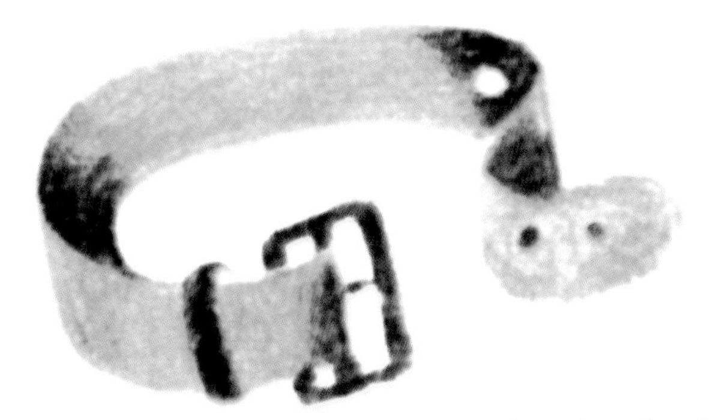

belt (ten) pásek
(ten) paa-sek

bench (ta) lavice
(tah) lah-vi-tse

bicycle (to) kolo
(to) ko-lo

binoculars (ten) dalekohled
(ten) dah-le-ko-hled

bird (ten) pták
(ten) ptaak

birdcage (ta) ptačí klec
(tah) ptah-chee klets

black **černý** *cher-nee*

blocks **(ty) kostky** *(ti) kost-ki*

blossom **(ten) květ** *(ten) kvyet*

blue **modrý** *mod-ree*

boat **(ten) člun** *(ten) chlun*

bone **(ta) kost** *(tah) kost*

book **(tah) kniha**
(tah) knyi-hah

boot **(ta) holínka**
(tah) ho-leen-kah

bottle **(ta) láhev**
(tah) laa-hef

bowl **(ta) mísa**
(tah) mee-sah

boy **(ten) chlapec**
(ten) khlah-pets

bracelet **(ten) náramek**
(ten) naa-rah-mek

branch (ta) větev
(tah) vye-tef

bread (ten) chléb
(ten) khleb

breakfast (ta) snídaně
(tah) snyee-dah-nye

bridge (ten) most
(ten) most

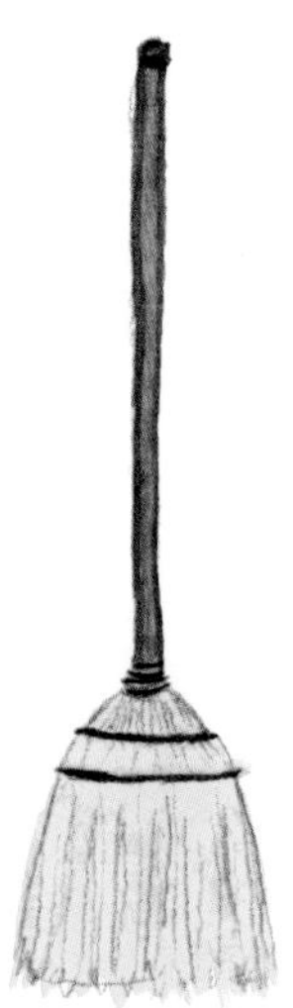

broom (to) koště
(to) kosh-tye

brother (ten) bratr
(ten) brah-tr

brown hnědý
hnye-dee

brush (ten) kartáč
(ten) kahr-taach

bucket (ten) kbelík
(ten) kbe-leek

bulletin board (ta) vývěska
(tah) vee-vyes-kah

bumblebee (ten) čmelák
(ten) chme-laak

butterfly (ten) motýl
(ten) mo-teel

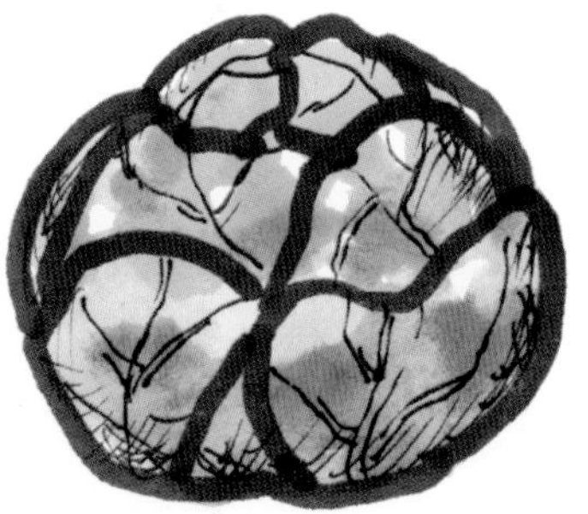

cab **(to) taxi**
(to) tah-ksi

cabbage **(to) zelí**
(to) ze-lee

cactus **(ten) kaktus**
(ten) kahk-tus

café **(ta) kavárna**
(tah) kah-vaar-nah

cake **(ten) dort**
(ten) dort

camel **(ten) velbloud**
(ten) vel-blowd

camera **(ten) fotoaparát**
(ten) fo-to-ah-pah-raat

candle **(ta) svíčka**
(tah) sveech-kah

candy **(to) cukroví**
(to) tsu-kro-vee

canoe **(ta) kánoe**
(tah) kaa-no-ye

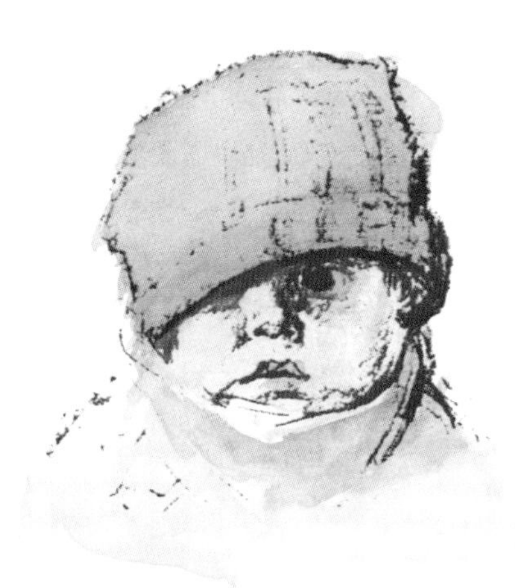

cap **(ta) čepice**
(tah) che-pi-tse

captain **(ten) kapitán**
(ten) kah-pi-taan

car **(to) auto**
(to) aw-to

card **(ta) karta**
(tah) kahr-tah

carpet **(ten) koberec**
(ten) ko-be-rets

carrot **(ta) mrkev**
(tah) mr-kev

(to) carry **nést**
nest

castle **(ten) hrad**
(ten) hrahd

cat (ta) kočka
(tah) koch-kah

cave (ta) jeskyně
(tah) yes-ki-nye

chair (ta) židle
(tah) zhid-le

cheese (ten) sýr
(ten) seer

cherry (ta) třešeň
(tah) trzhe-shen'

chimney (ten) komín
(ten) koh-meen

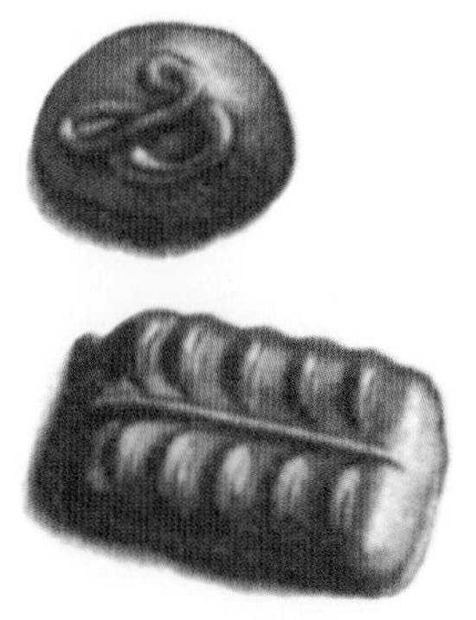

chocolate (ta) čokoláda
(tah) cho-ko-laa-dah

Christmas tree (ten) Vánoční stromek
(ten) vaa-noch-nyee stro-mek

circus (ten) cirkus
(ten) tsir-kus

(to) climb vylézt
vi-lest

cloud (ten) mrak
(ten) mrahk

clown (ten) šašek
(ten) shah-shek

coach **(ten) kočár**
(ten) ko-chaar

coat **(ten) kabát**
(ten) kah-baat

coconut **(ten) kokos**
(ten) ko-kos

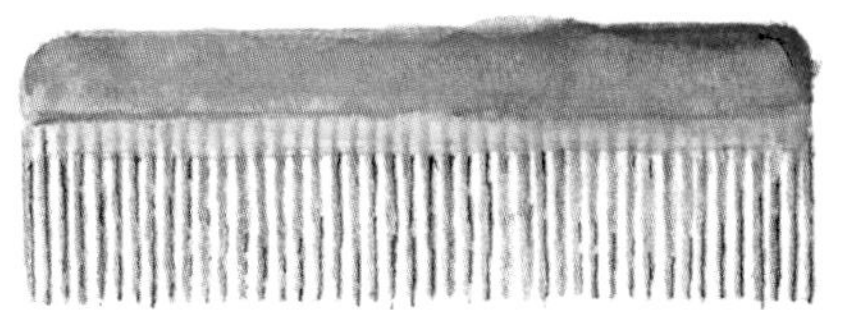

comb **(ten) hřeben**
(ten) hrzhe-ben

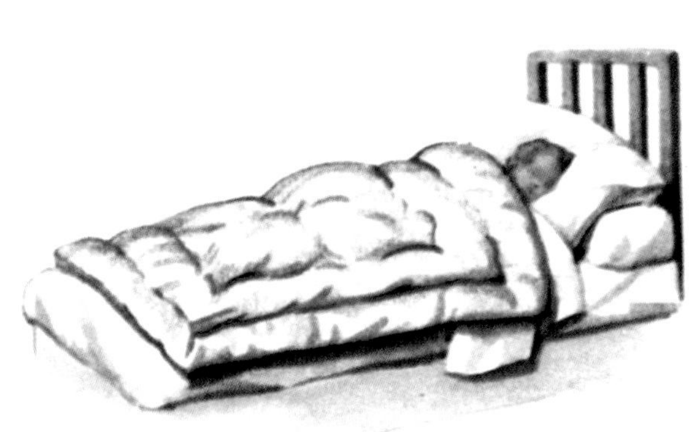

comforter **(ta) peřina**
(tah) pe-rzhi-nah

compass **(ten) kompas**
(ten) kom-pahs

(to) cook

vařit
vah-rzhit

cork

(ten) zátka
(tah) zaat-kah

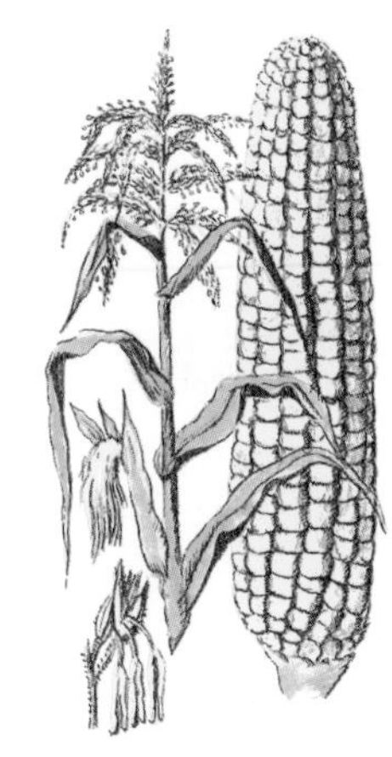

corn

(ta) kukuřice
(tah) ku-ku-rzhi-tse

cow

(ta) kráva
(tah) kraa-vah

cracker

(ta) sušenka
(tah) su-shen-kah

cradle

(ta) kolébka
(tah) ko-lehb-kah

(to) crawl — **lézt** *lest*

(to) cross — 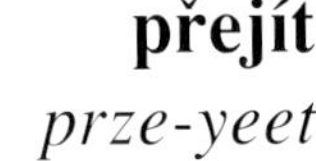
přejít *prze-yeet*

crown — **(ta) koruna** *(tah) ko-ru-nah*

(to) cry — **plakat** *plah-kaht*

cucumber — **(ta) okurka** *(tah) o-kur-kah*

curtain — **(ta) záclona** *(tah) zaats-lo-nah*

(to) dance — **tančit**
tahn-chit

dandelion — **(ta) pampeliška**
(tah) pahm-pe-lish-kah

MAY						
M	T	W	T	F	S	S
		1	2	3	4	5
6	7	8	9	10	11	12
13	14	15	16	17	18	19
20	21	22	23	24	25	26
27	28	29	30	31		

date — **(to) datum**
(to) dah-tum

deer — **(ten) jelen**
(ten) ye-len

desert — **(ta) poušt’**
(tah) powsht’

desk — **(ten) psací stůl**
(ten) psah-tsee stool

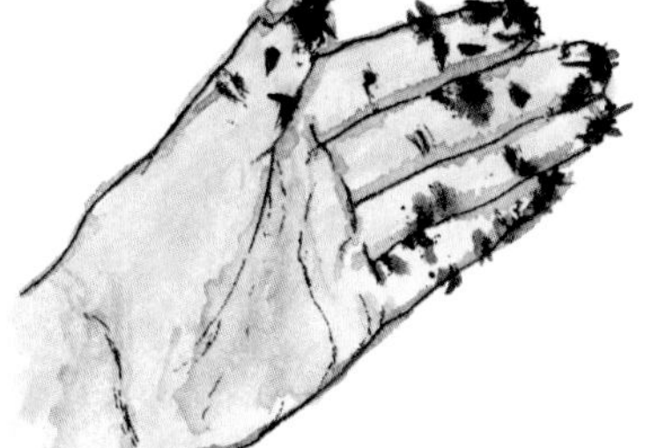

dirty — **špinavý**
shpi-nah-vee

dog **(ten) pes**

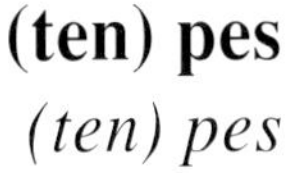

(ten) pes

doghouse **(ta) psí bouda**
(tah) psee bow-dah

doll **(ta) panenka**
(tah) pah-nen-kah

dollhouse **(ten) domeček pro panenky**
(ten) do-me-chek pro pah-nen-ki

dolphin **(ten) delfín**
(ten) del-feen

donkey **(ten) osel**
(ten) o-sel

dragon **(ten) drak**
(ten) drahk

dragonfly (ta) vážka
(tah) vaazh-kah

(to) draw kreslit
kres-lit

dress (ty) šaty
(ti) shah-ti

(to) drink napít se
nah-peet se

drum (ten) buben
(ten) bu-ben

duck (ta) kachna
(tah) kakh-nah

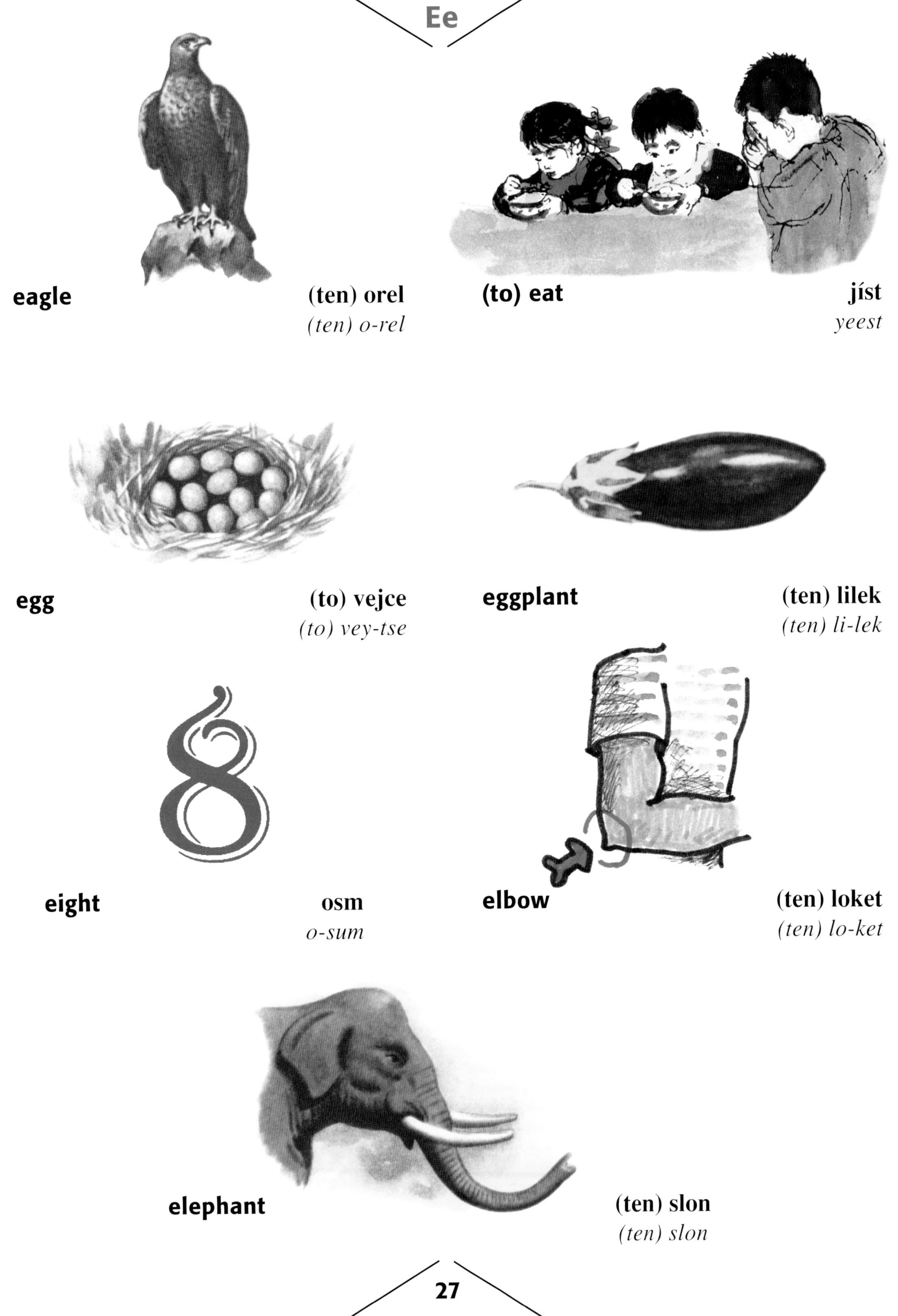

eagle **(ten) orel**
(ten) o-rel

(to) eat **jíst**
yeest

egg **(to) vejce**
(to) vey-tse

eggplant **(ten) lilek**
(ten) li-lek

eight **osm**
o-sum

elbow **(ten) loket**
(ten) lo-ket

elephant **(ten) slon**
(ten) slon

empty prázdný
praaz-dnee

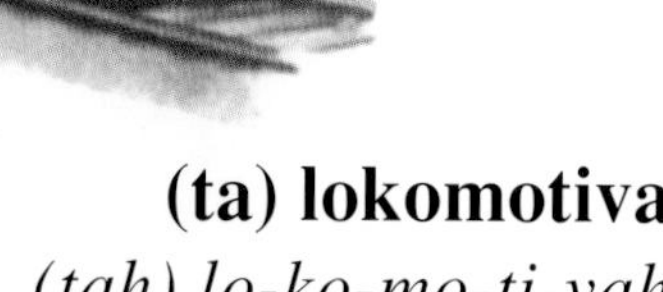

engine (ta) lokomotiva
(tah) lo-ko-mo-ti-vah

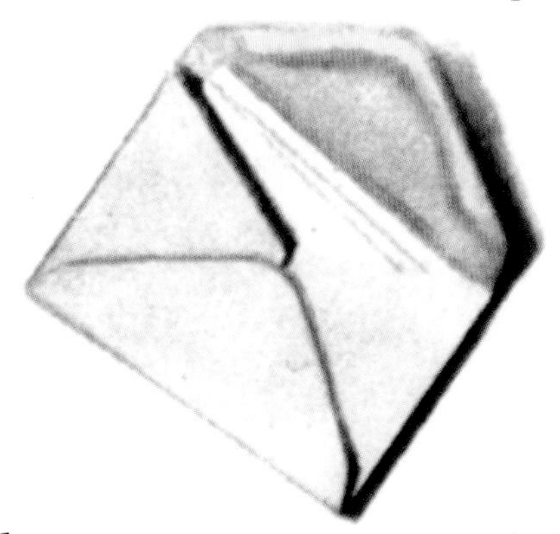

envelope (ta) obálka
(tah) o-baal-kah

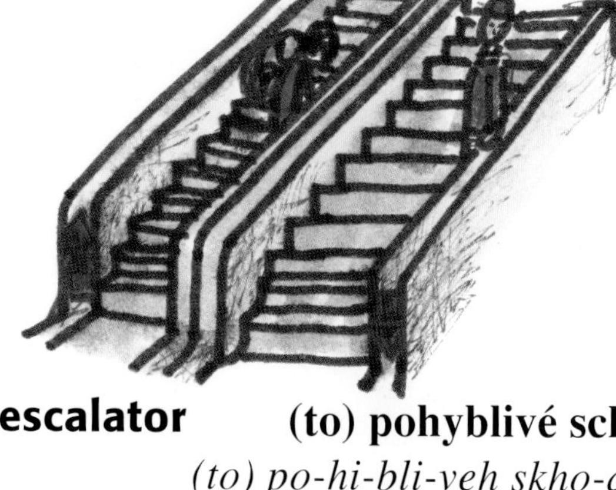

escalator (to) pohyblivé schodiště
(to) po-hi-bli-veh skho-dish-tye

Eskimo (ten) Eskymák
(ten) es-ki-maak

(to) explore prozkoumat
proz-kow-mat

eye (to) oko
(to) o-ko

face **(ten) obličej**
(ten) ob-li-chey

fan **(ten) ventilátor**
(ten) ven-ti-laa-tor

father **(ten) otec**
(ten) o-tets

fear **(ten) strach**
(ten) strakh

feather **(to) pero**
(to) pe-ro

(to) feed **krmit**
kr-mit

fence **(ten) plot**
(ten) plot

fern **(ta) kapradina**
(tah) kah-prah-dyi-nah

field **(to) pole**
(toh) po-le

field mouse **(ten) hraboš polní**
(ten) hrah-bosh pol-nyee

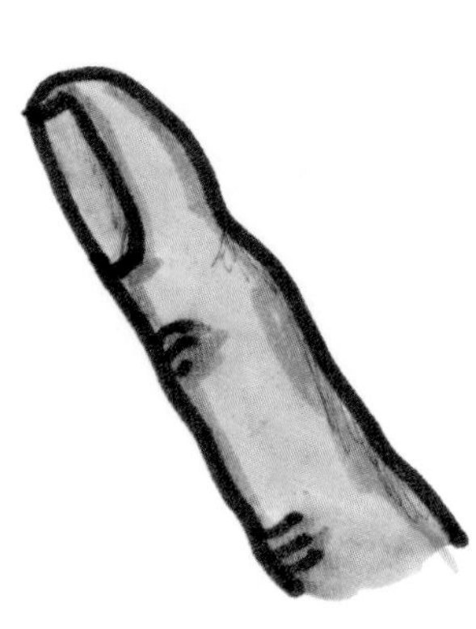

finger **(ten) prst**
(ten) prst

fir tree **(ta) jedle**
(tah) yed-le

fire **(ten) oheň**
(ten) oh-hen'

fish **(ta) ryba**
(tah) ri-bah

(to) fish **lovit ryby**
lo-vit ri-bi

fist **(ta) pěst**
(tah) pyest

five **pět**
pyet

flag **(tah) vlajka**
(tah) vlahy-kah

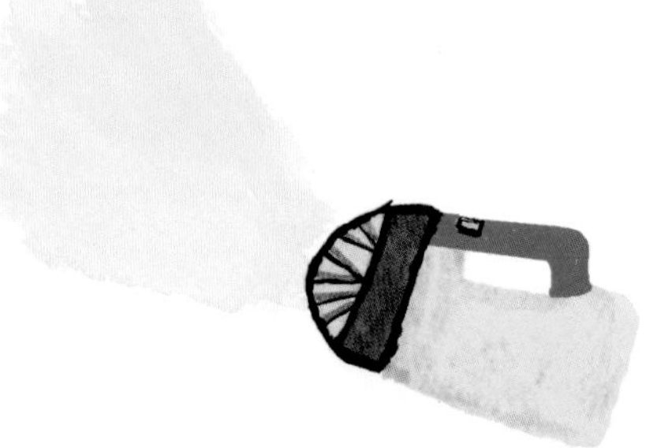

flashlight — **(ta) baterka**
(tah) bah-ter-kah

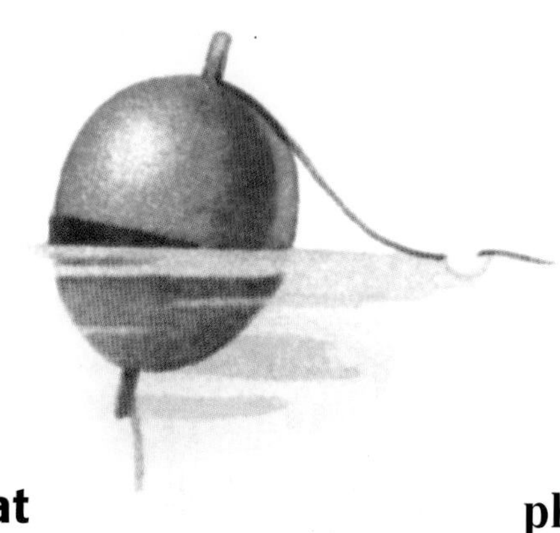

(to) float — **plout**
plowt

flower — **(ta) květina**
(tah) kvye-tyi- nah

(to) fly — **letět**
le-tyet

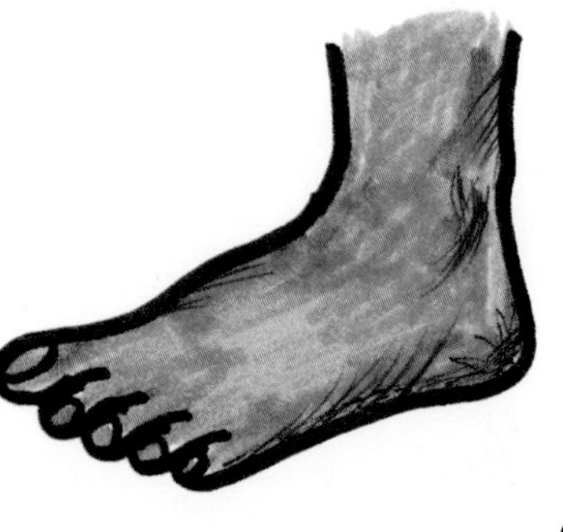

foot — **(ta) noha**
(tah) no-hah

fork — **(ta) vidlička**
(tah) vid-lich-kah

fountain —  **(ta) fontána**
(tah) fon-taa-nah

four čtyři
chti-rzhi

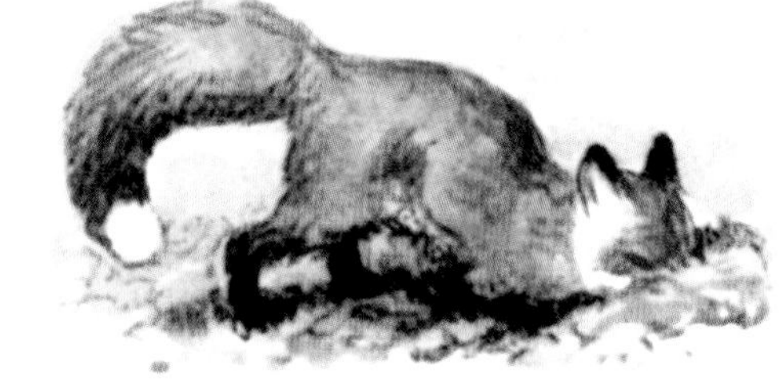

fox (ta) liška
(tah) lish-kah

frame (ten) rám
(ten) raam

friend (ten) kamarád
(ten) kah-mah-raad

frog (ta) žába
(tah) zhaah-bah

fruit (to) ovoce
(toh) o-vo-tse

furniture (ten) nábytek
(ten) naa-bi-tek

garden (ta) zahrada
(tah) zah-hrah-dah

gate (ta) brána
(tah) braa-nah

(to) gather sbírat
sbee-raht

geranium (ta) pelargonie
(tah) pe-lahr-go-ni-ye

giraffe (ta) žirafa
(tah) zhi-rah-fah

girl (ta) dívka
(tah) dyeev-kah

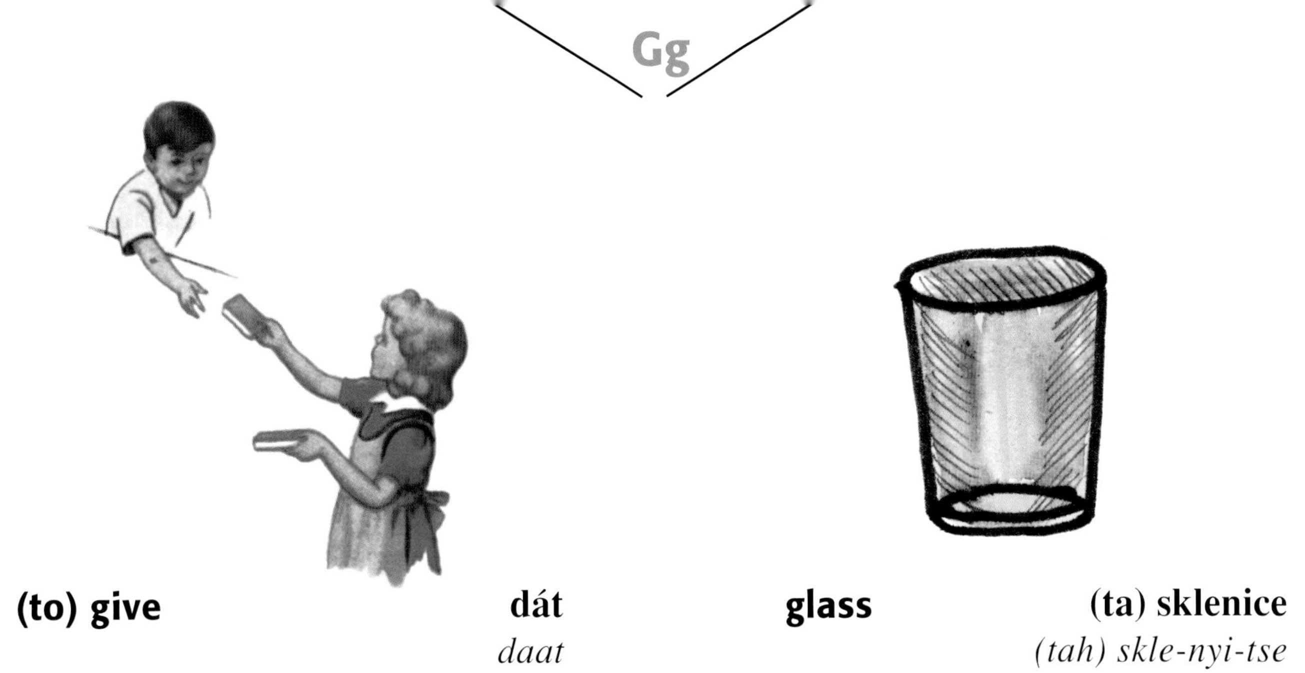

(to) give **dát**
daat

glass **(ta) sklenice**
(tah) skle-nyi-tse

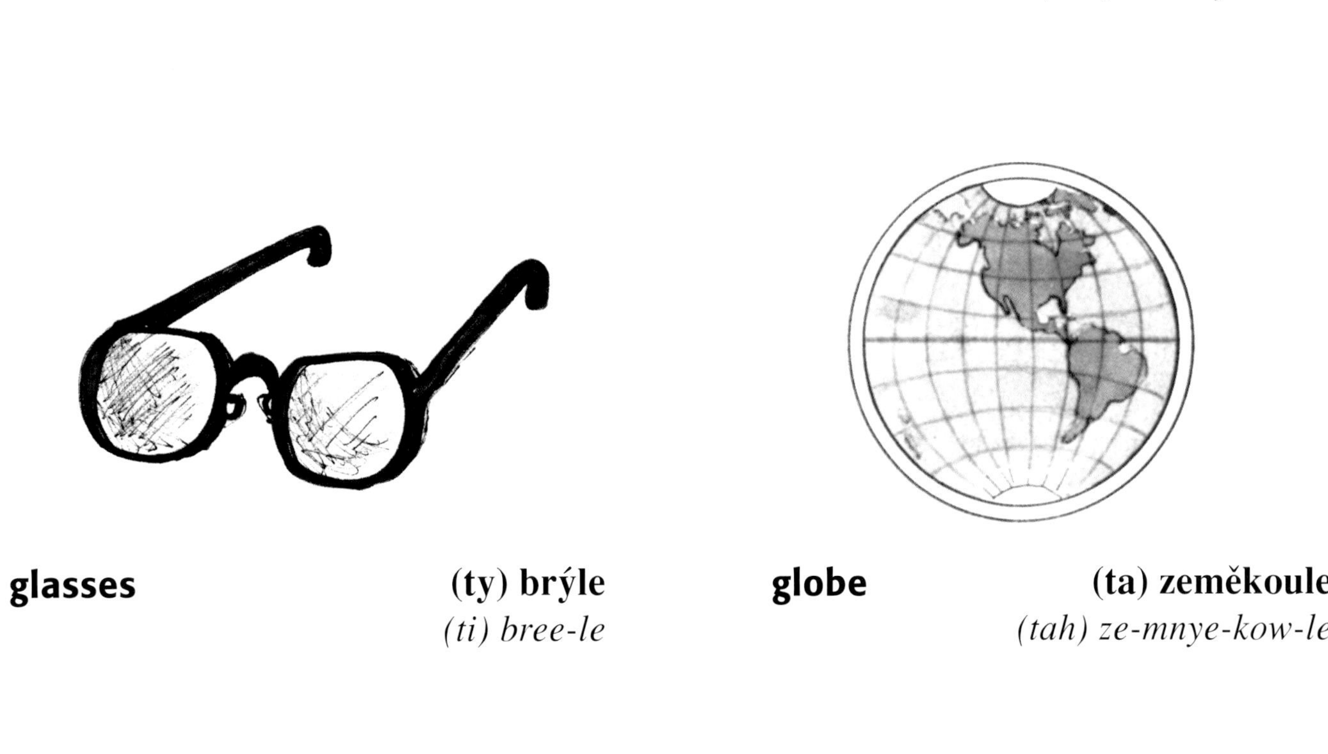

glasses **(ty) brýle**
(ti) bree-le

globe **(ta) zeměkoule**
(tah) ze-mnye-kow-le

glove **(ta) rukavice**
(tah) ru-kah-vi-tse

goat **(ta) koza**
(tah) ko-zah

goldfish (ta) zlatá rybka
(tah) zlah-taa rib-kah

"Good Night" "Dobrou Noc"
"Dob-row Nots"

"Good-bye" "Nashledanou"
"Nah-skhleh-dah-now"

goose (ta) husa
(tah) hu-sah

grandfather (ten) dědeček
(ten) dye-de-chek

grandmother (ta) babička
(tah) bah-bich-kah

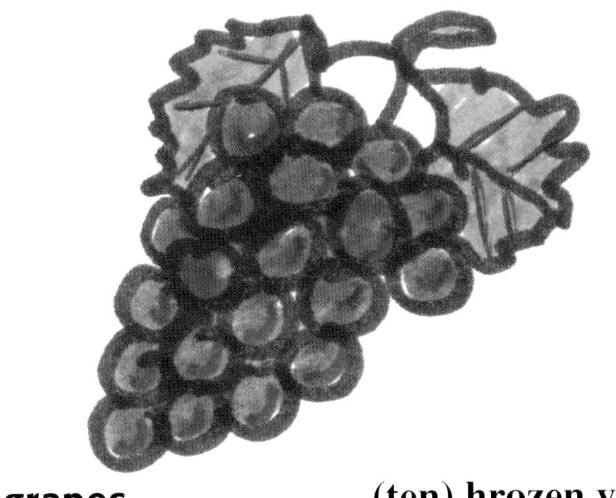

grapes **(ten) hrozen vína**
(ten) hro-zen vee-nah

grasshopper **(ta) kobylka**
(tah) ko-bil-kah

green **zelený**
ze-le-nee

greenhouse **(ten) skleník**
(ten) skle-nyeek

guitar **(ta) kytara**
(tah) ki-tah-rah

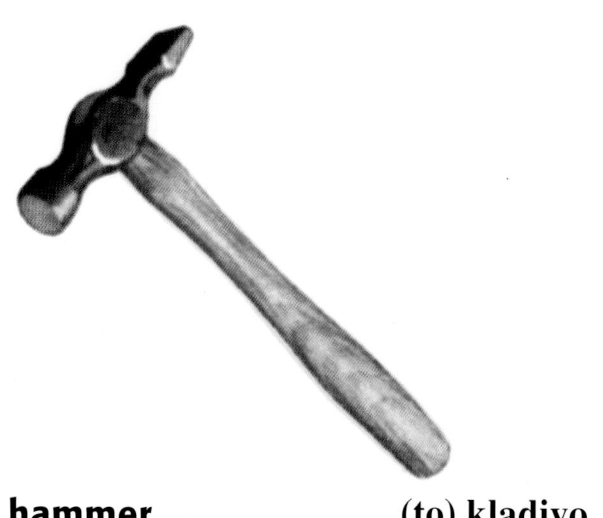

hammer (to) kladivo
(to) klah-dyi-vo

hammock (ta) sít'ová houpačka
(tah) see-tyo-vaa how-pach-kah

hamster (ten) křeček
(ten) krzhe-chek

hand (ta) ruka
(tah) ru-kah

handbag (ta) kabelka
(tah) kah-bel-kah

handkerchief (ten) kapesník
(ten) kah-pes-nyeek

harvest **(ty) žně**
(ti) zhnye

hat **(ten) klobouk**
(ten) klo-bowk

hay **(to) seno**
(to) se-no

headdress **(ta) čelenka**
(tah) che-len-kah

heart **(to) srdce**
(to) sr-tse

hedgehog **(ten) ježek**
(ten) ye-zhek

hen **(ta) slepice**
(tah) sle-pi-tse

(to) hide **schovat se**
skho-vaht se

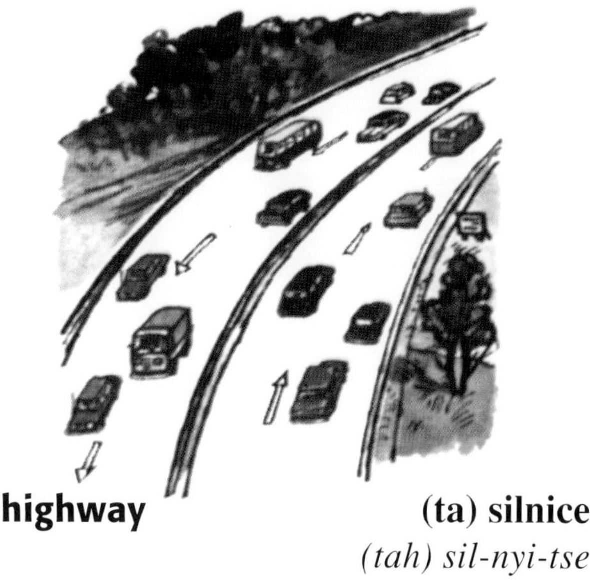

highway **(ta) silnice**
(tah) sil-nyi-tse

honey **(ten) med**
(ten) med

horns **(ty) rohy**
(ti) ro-hi

horse **(ten) kůň**
(ten) koon'

horseshoe **(ta) podkova**
(tah) pod-ko-vah

hourglass **(ty) přesýpací hodiny**
(ti) przhe-see-pah-tsee ho-dyi-ni

house **(ten) dům**
(ten) doom

(to) hug **obejmout**
o-bey-mowt

hydrant **(ten) hydrant**
(ten) hi-drahnt

ice cream (ta) zmrzlina
(tah) zmr-zli-nah

ice cubes (ty) kostky ledu
(ti) kost-ki le-du

ice-skating bruslit
brus-lit

instrument nástroj
naa-stroy

iris (ten) kosatec
(ten) ko-sah-tets

iron (ta) žehlička
(tah) zhe-hlich-kah

island (ten) ostrov
(ten) o-strov

jacket **(ten) kabátek**
(ten) kah-baa-tek

jam **(ta) marmeláda**
(tah) mar-me-laa-dah

jigsaw puzzle **(ta) skládačka**
(tah) sklaa-dach-kah

jockey **(ten) žokej**
(ten) zho-key

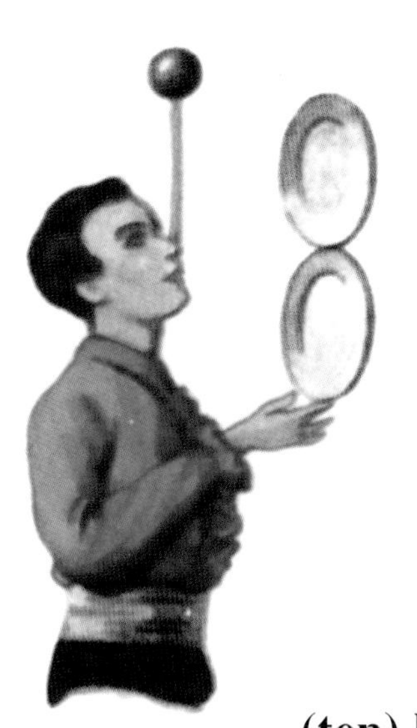

juggler **(ten) kejklíř**
(ten) key-kleerzh

(to) jump **skočit**
sko-chit

kangaroo (ten) klokan
(ten) klo-kahn

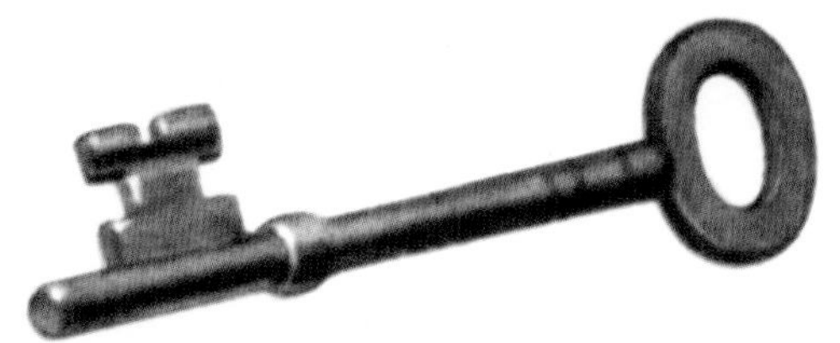

key (ten) klíč
(ten) kleech

kitten (to) kot'átko
(to) ko-tyaat-ko

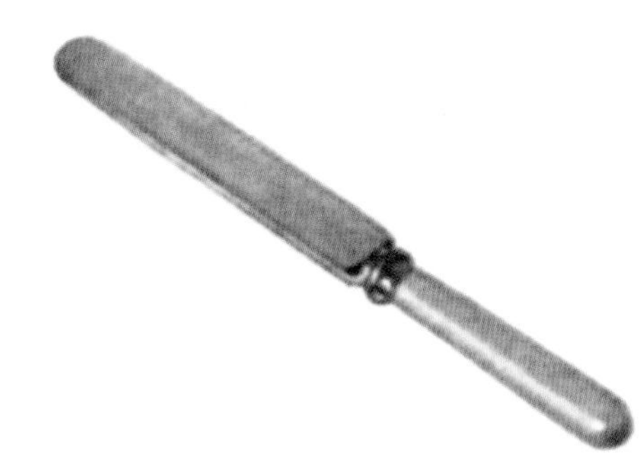

knife (ten) nůž
(ten) noozh

knight (ten) rytíř
(ten) ri-tyeerzh

(to) knit plést
plest

knot (ten) uzel
(ten) u-zel

koala bear (ten) medvídek koala
(ten) med-vee-dek ko-ah-lah

ladder (ten) žebřík
(ten) zheb-rzheek

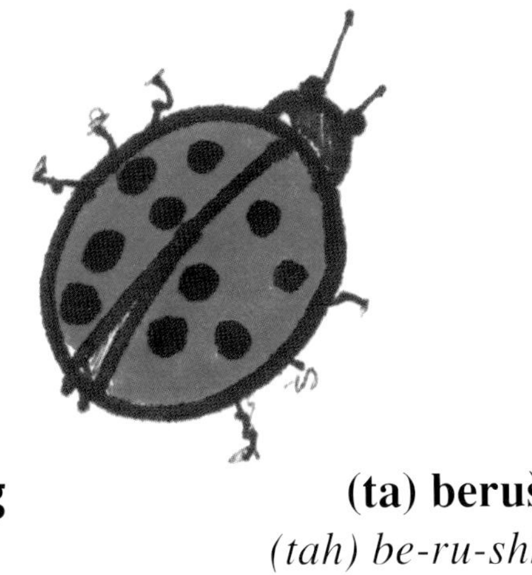

ladybug (ta) beruška
(tah) be-ru-shkah

lamb (ten) beránek
(ten) be-raa-nek

lamp (ta) lampa
(tah) lahm-pah

(to) lap lízat
lee-zaht

laughter (ten) smích
(ten) smeekh

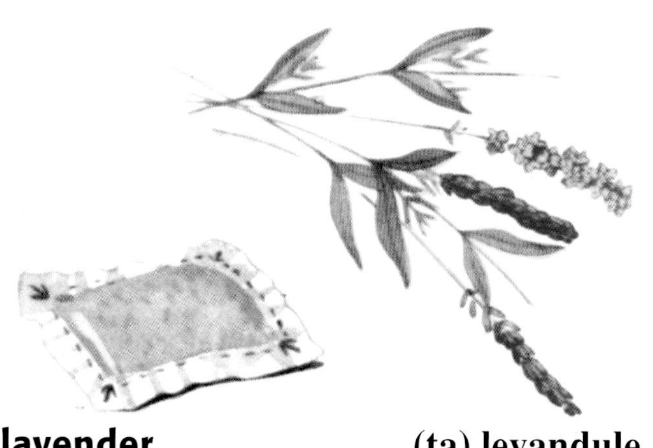

lavender (ta) levandule
(tah) le-vahn-du-le

lawn mower (ten) žací stroj na trávu
(ten) shah-tsee stroy na traa-vu

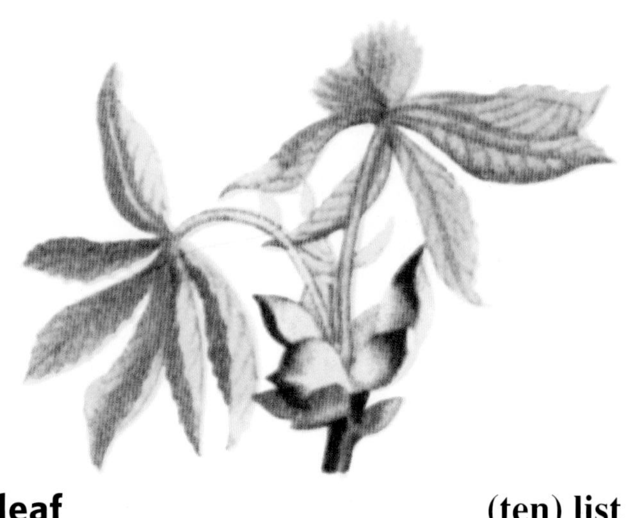

leaf (ten) list
(ten) list

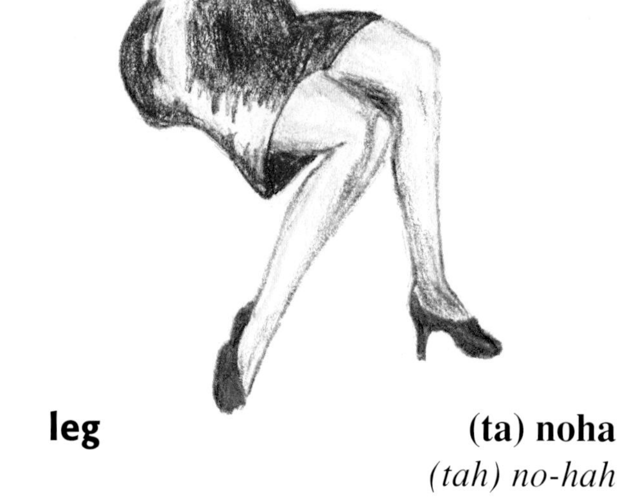

leg (ta) noha
(tah) no-hah

lemon (ten) citrón
(ten) tsi-trohn

lettuce (ten) hlávkový salát
(ten) hlaav-ko-vee sah-laat

lightbulb (ta) žárovka
(tah) zhaa-rov-kah

lighthouse (ten) maják
(ten) mah-yaak

lilac (ten) šeřík
(ten) she-rzheek

lion (ten) lev
(ten) lef

(to) listen poslouchat
poh-slow-khat

lobster (ta) langusta
(tah) lahn-gus-tah

lock **(ten) zámek**
(ten) zaa-mek

lovebird **malý papoušek**
mah-lee pah-pow-shek

luggage **(ty) zavazadla**
(ti) zah-vah-zahd-lah

lumberjack **(ten) dřevorubec**
(ten) drzhe-vo-ru-bets

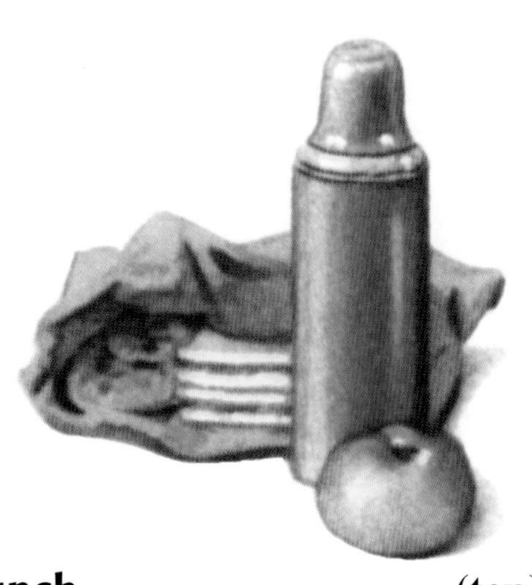

lunch **(ten) oběd**
(ten) o-byed

lynx **(ten) rys**
(ten) ris

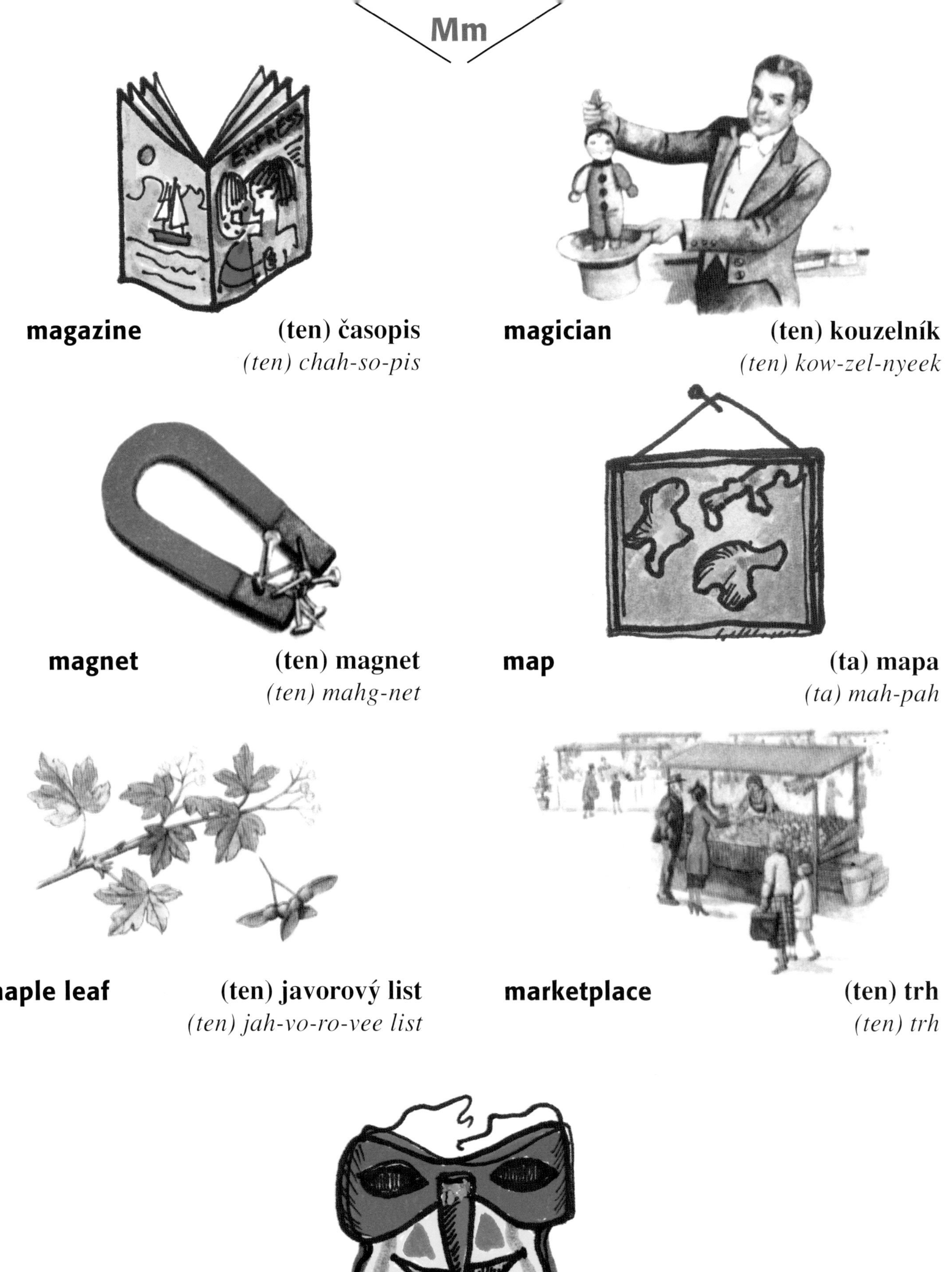

magazine (ten) časopis
(ten) chah-so-pis

magician (ten) kouzelník
(ten) kow-zel-nyeek

magnet (ten) magnet
(ten) mahg-net

map (ta) mapa
(ta) mah-pah

maple leaf (ten) javorový list
(ten) jah-vo-ro-vee list

marketplace (ten) trh
(ten) trh

mask (ta) maska
(tah) mah-skah

messy — **nepořádný**
ne-po-rzhaa-dnee

milkman — **(ten) mlékař**
(ten) mle-karzh

mirror — **(to) zrcadlo**
(toh) zr-tsah-dlo

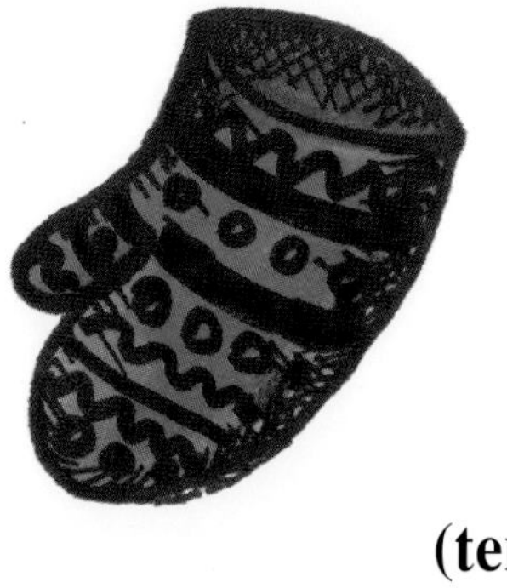

mitten — **(ten) palčák**
(ten) pahl-chaak

money — **(ty) peníze**
(ti) pe-nyee-ze

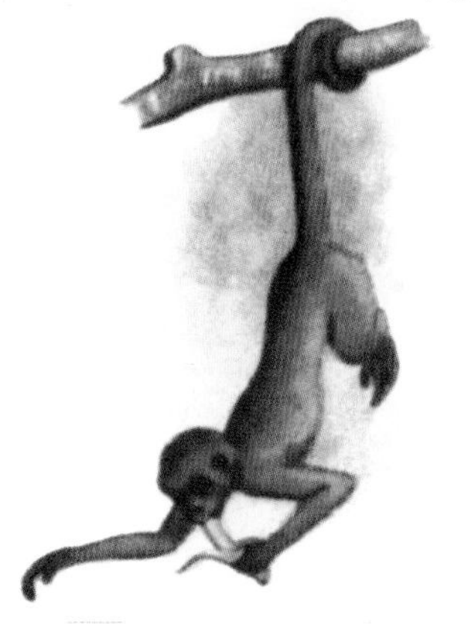

monkey — **(ta) opice**
(tah) o-pi-tse

moon — **(ten) měsíc**
(ten) mnye-seets

mother **(ta) matka**
(tah) maht-kah

mountain **(ta) hora**
(tah) ho-rah

mouse **(ta) myška**
(tah) mish-kah

mouth **(ta) pusa**
(tah) pu-sah

mushroom **(ta) houba**
(tah) how-bah

music **(ta) hudba**
(tah) hud-bah

naked **nahý**
nah-hee

necklace **(ten) náhrdelník**
(ten) naa-hr-del-nyeek

needle **(ta) jehla**
(tah) ye-hlah

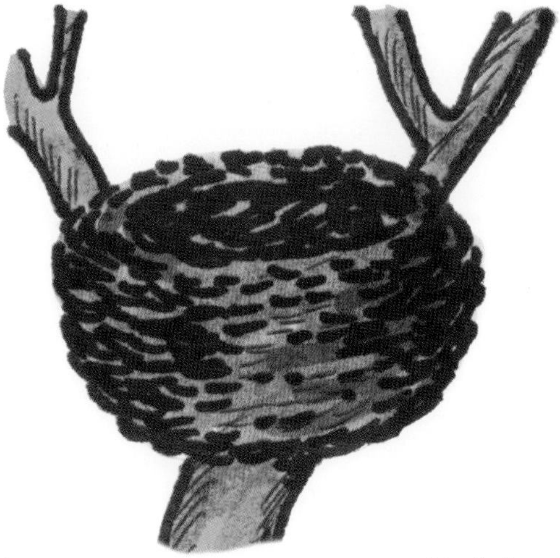

nest **(to) hnízdo**
(toh) hnyee-zdo

newspaper **(ty) noviny**
(ti) no-vi-ni

nightingale **(ten) slavík**
(ten) slah-veek

nine **devět**
de-vyet

notebook **(ten) sešit**
(ten) se-shit

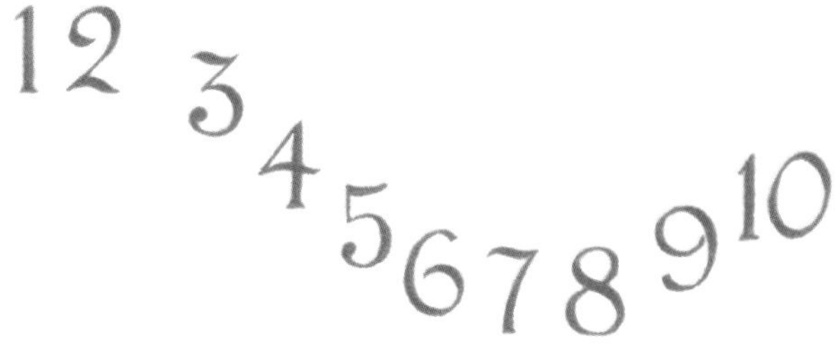

number **(to) číslo**
(to) chee-slo

nut **(ten) ořech**
(ten) o-rzhekh

oar (to) veslo
(to) ves-lo

ocean liner (ta) zaoceánská lod'
(tah) zah-o-tse-aan-skaah lod'

old starý
stah-ree

one jeden
ye-den

onion (ta) cibule
(tah) tsi-bu-le

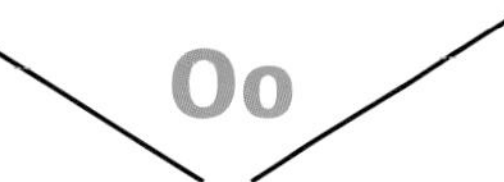

open otevřeno
o-tev-rzhe-no

orange (ten) pomeranč
(ten) po-me-rahnch

ostrich (ten) pštros
(ten) psh-tros

owl (ta) sova
(tah) so-vah

ox ten) vůl
(ten) vool

padlock (ten) visací zámek
(ten) vi-sah-tsee zaa-mek

paint (ta) barva
(tah) bahr-vah

painter (ten) malíř
(ten) mah-leerzh

pajamas (to) pyžama
(to) pi-zhah-mah

palm tree (ta) palma
(tah) pahl-mah

paper (ten) papír
(ten) pah-peer

parachute (ten) padák
(ten) pah-daak

park (ten) park
(ten) pahrk

parrot (ten) papoušek
(ten) pah-pow-shek

passport (ten) cestovní pas
(ten) tses-tov-nyee pahs

patch (ta) záplata
(tah) zaa-plah-tah

path (ta) pěšina
(tah) pye-shi-nah

peach (ta) broskev
(tah) bros-kev

pear (ta) hruška
(tah) hrush-kah

pebble (ten) oblázek
(ten) o-blaa-zek

(to) peck zobat
zo-baht

(to) peel loupat
low-paht

pelican (ten) pelikán
(ten) pe-li-kaan

pencil (ta) tužka
(tah) tuzh-kah

penguin (ten) tučňák
(ten) tuch-nyaak

people (ti) lidé
(ti) li-deh

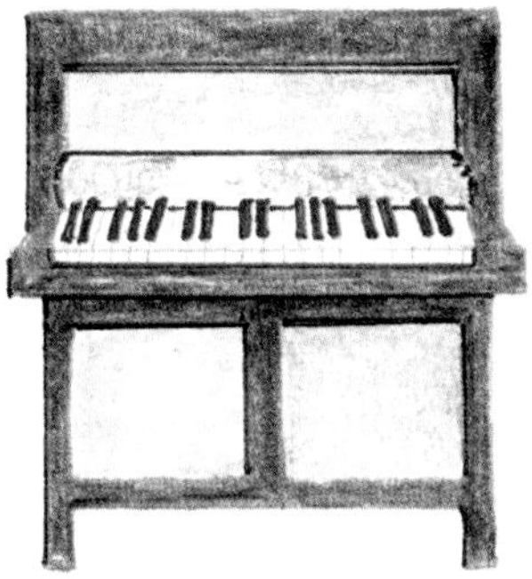

piano **(to) piano**
(toh) pi-yah-no

pickle **(ta) kyselá okurka**
(tah) ki-se-laa o-kur-kah

pie **(ten) koláč**
(ten) ko-laach

pig **(to) prase**
(toh) prah-se

pigeon **(ten) holub**
(ten) ho-lub

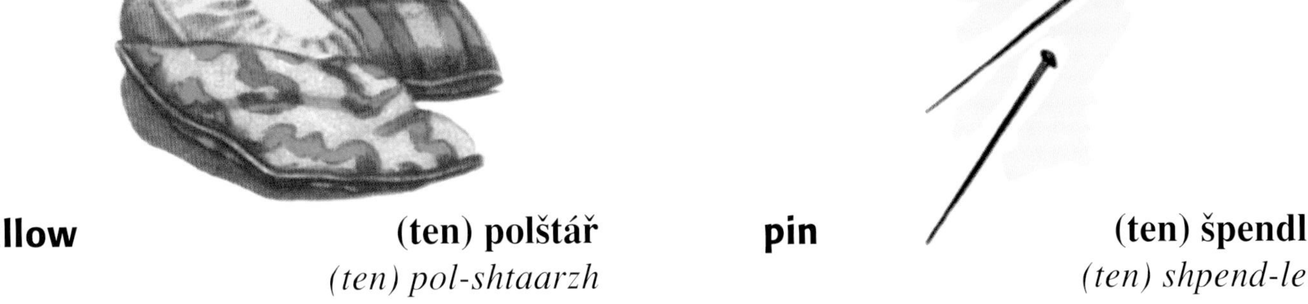

pillow **(ten) polštář**
(ten) pol-shtaarzh

pin **(ten) špendlík**
(ten) shpend-leek

pine (ta) sosna
(tah) sos-nah

pineapple (ten) ananas
(ten) ah-nah-nahs

pit (ta) pecka
(tah) pets-kah

pitcher (ten) džbán
(ten) dzh-baan

plate (ten) talíř
(ten) tah-leerzh

platypus (ten) ptakopysk
(ten) ptah-ko-pisk

(to) play — **hrát si**
hraat si

plum — **(ta) švestka**
(tah) shvest-kah

polar bear — **(ten) lední medvěd**
(ten) led-nyee med-vyed

pony — **(ten) pony**
(ten) po-ni

pot — **(ten) hrnec**
(ten) hr-nets

potato — **(ten) brambor**
(ten) brahm-bor

(to) pour **lít**
leet

present **(ten) dárek**
(ten) daa-rek

(to) pull **tahat**
tah-hat

pumpkin **(ta) dýně**
(tah) dee-nye

puppy **(to) štěně**
(to) shtye-nye

Qq

queen **(ta) královna**
(tah) kraa-lov-nah

rabbit **(ten) králík**
(ten) kraa-leek

raccoon **(ten) mýval**
(ten) mee-vahl

racket **(ta) tenisová raketa**
(tah) te-ni-so-vaa rah-ke-tah

radio **(to) rádio**
(to) raa-di-yo

radish **(ta) ředkvička**
(tah) rzhed-kvich-kah

raft (ten) prám
(ten) praam

rain (ten) déšť
(ten) desht'

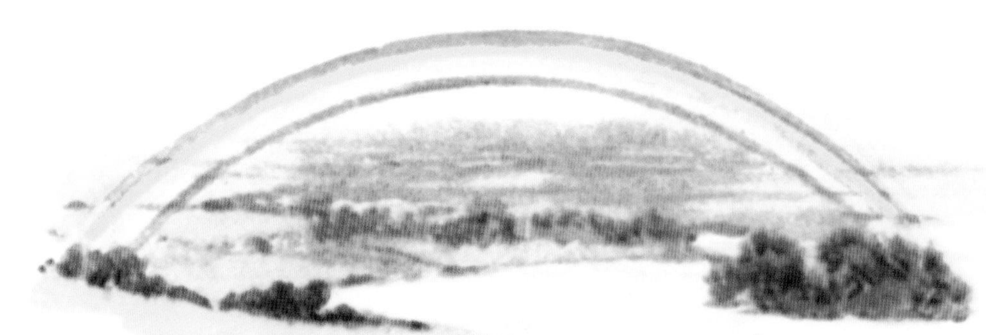

rainbow (ta) duha
(tah) du-hah

raincoat (ten) nepromokavý plášť
(ten) ne-pro-mo-kah-vee plaasht'

raspberry (ta) malina
(tah) mah-li-nah

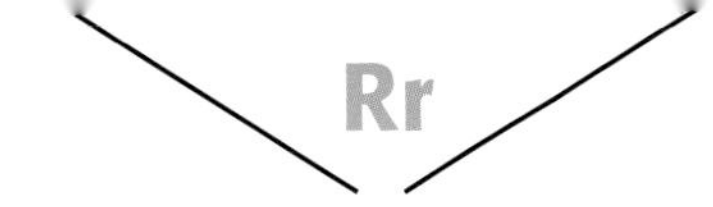

(to) read **číst**
cheest

red **červený**
cher-ve-nee

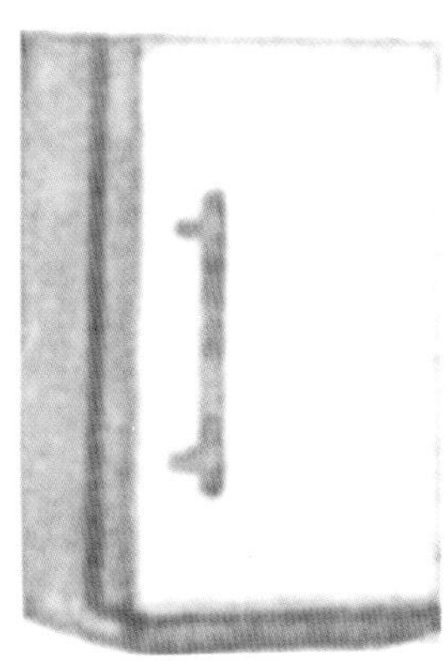

refrigerator **(ta) lednička**
(tah) led-nyich-kah

rhinoceros **(ten) nosorožec**
(ten) no-so-ro-zhets

ring **(ten) prsten**
(ten) prs-ten

(to) ring **zvonit**
zvo-nyit

river **(ta) řeka**
(tah) rzhe-kah

road **(ta) cesta**
(tah) tses-tah

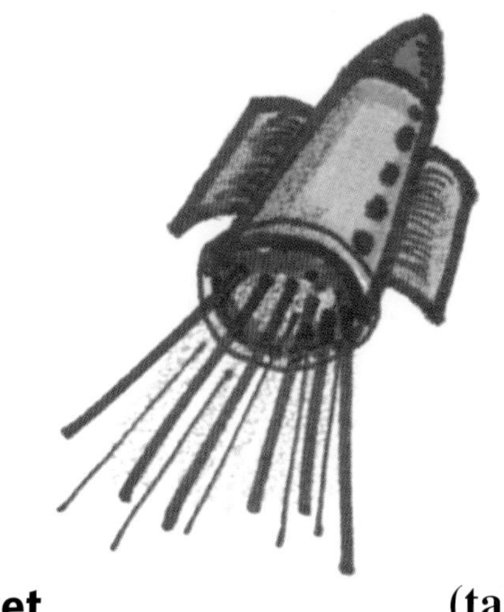

rocket **(ta) raketa**
(tah) rah-ke-tah

roof **(ta) střecha**
(tah) strzhe-khah

rooster **(ten) kohout**
(ten) ko-howt

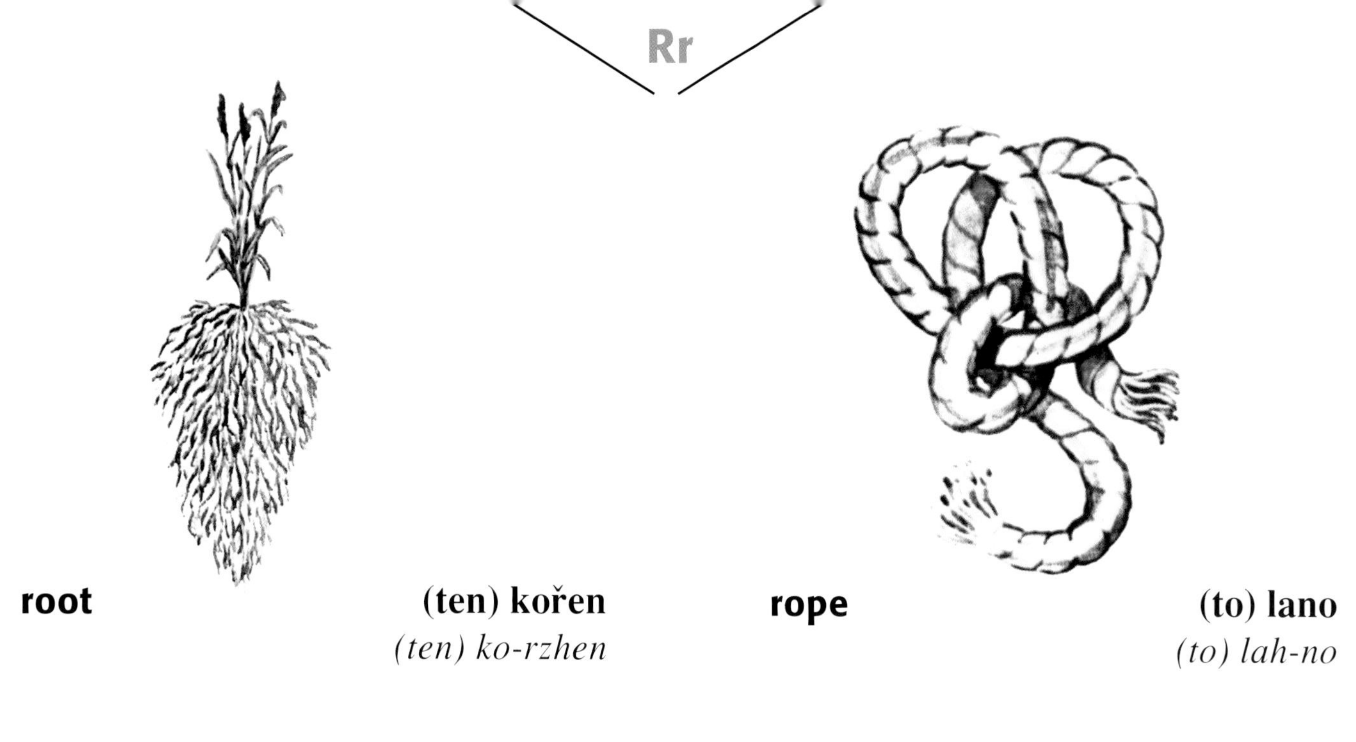

root **(ten) kořen**
(ten) ko-rzhen

rope **(to) lano**
(to) lah-no

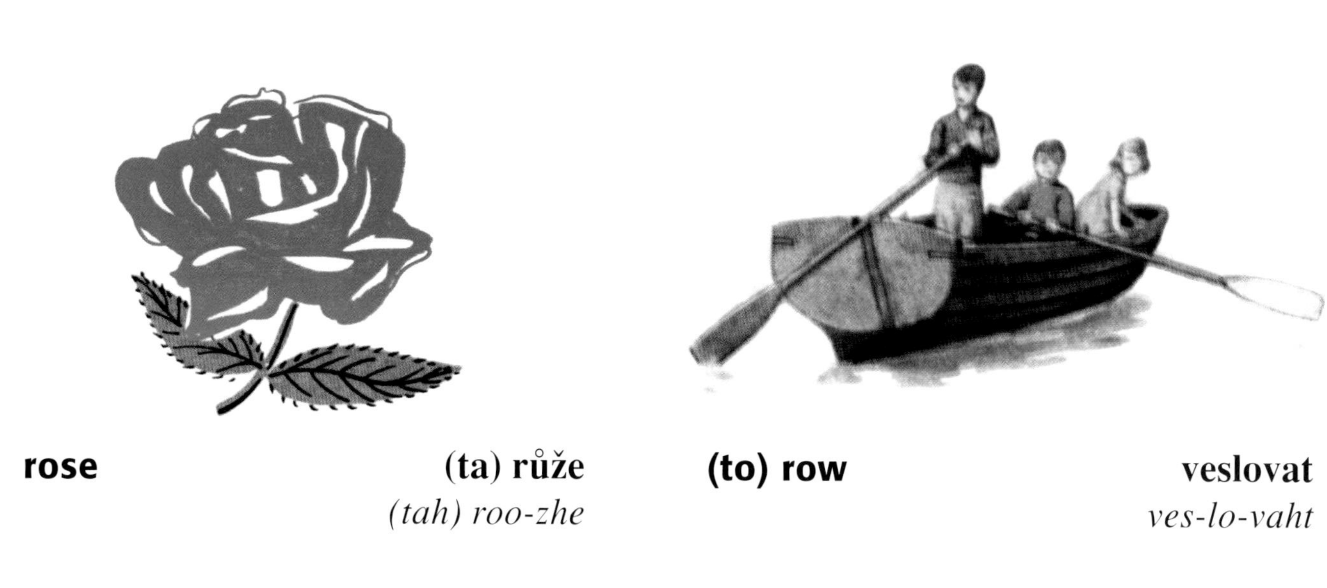

rose **(ta) růže**
(tah) roo-zhe

(to) row **veslovat**
ves-lo-vaht

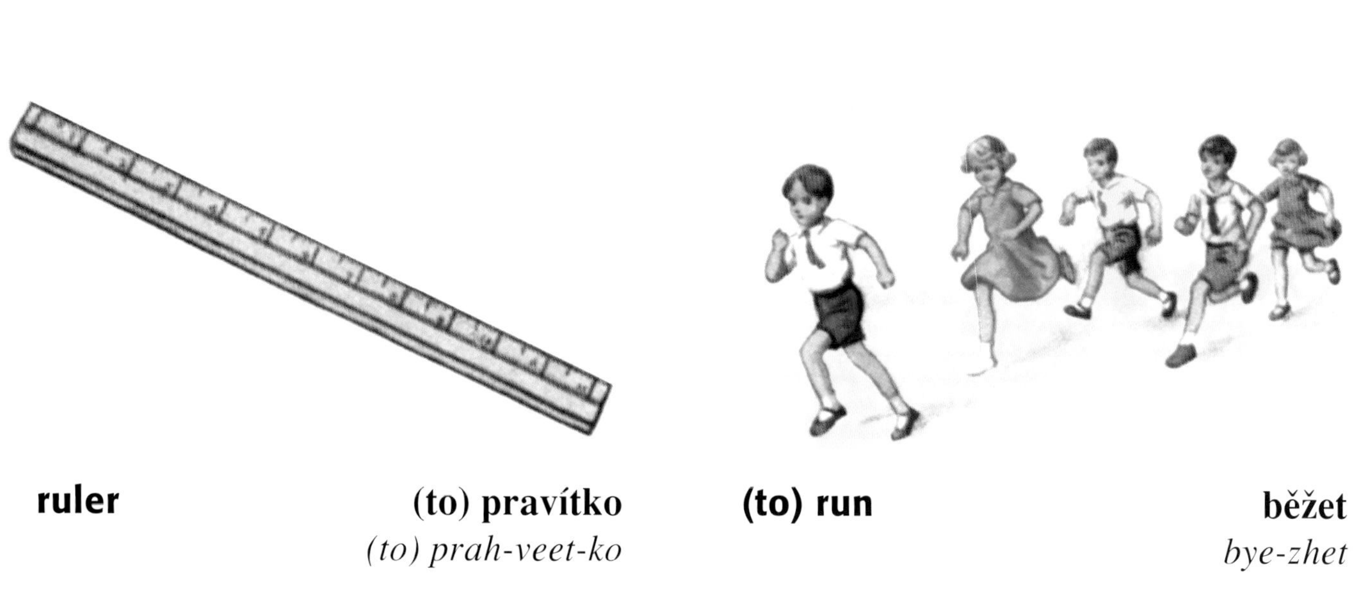

ruler **(to) pravítko**
(to) prah-veet-ko

(to) run **běžet**
bye-zhet

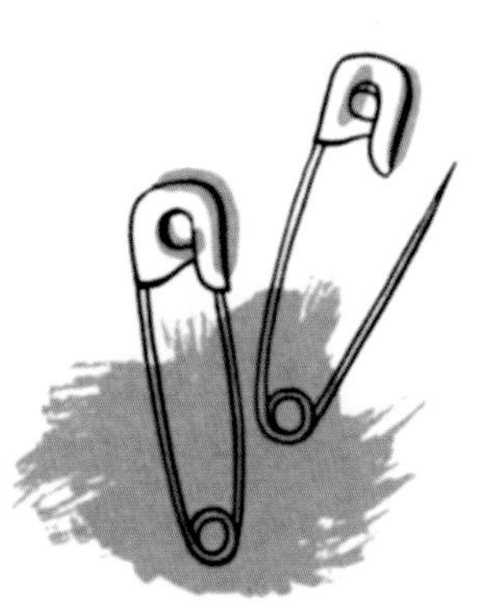

safety pin (ten) zavírací špendlík
(ten) zah-vee-rah-tsee shpend-leek

(to) sail plout
plowt

sailor (ten) námořník
(ten) naa-morzh-nyeek

salt (ta) sůl
(tah) sool

scarf (ten) šátek
(ten) shaa-tek

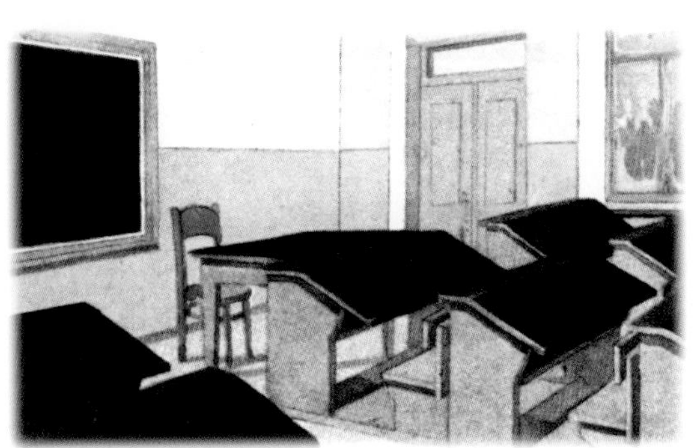

school (ta) škola
(tah) shko-lah

scissors (ty) nůžky
(ti) noozh-ki

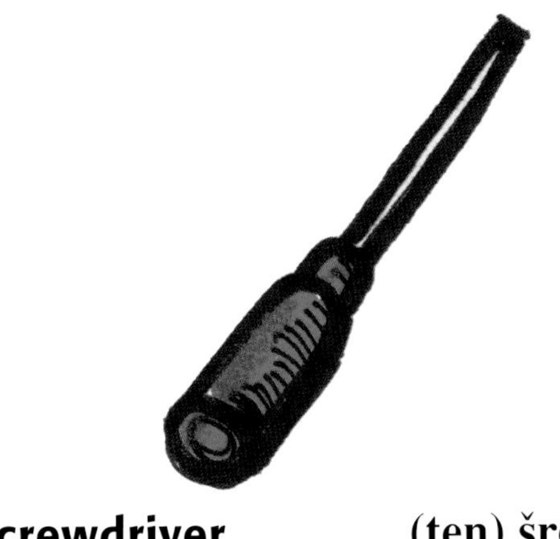

screwdriver (ten) šroubovák
(ten) shrow-bo-vaak

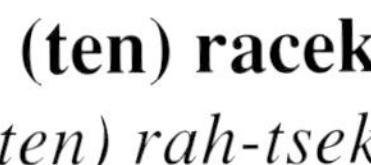

seagull (ten) racek
(ten) rah-tsek

seesaw (tah) houpačka
(tah) how-pach-kah

seven sedm
se-dum

(to) sew ušít
u-sheet

shark (ten) žralok
(ten) zhrah-lok

sheep (ta) ovce
(tah) ov-tse

shell (ta) mušle
(tah) mush-le

shepherd (ten) pastýř
(ten) pas-teerzh

ship (ta) lod'
(tah) lod'

shirt (ta) košile
(tah) ko-shi-le

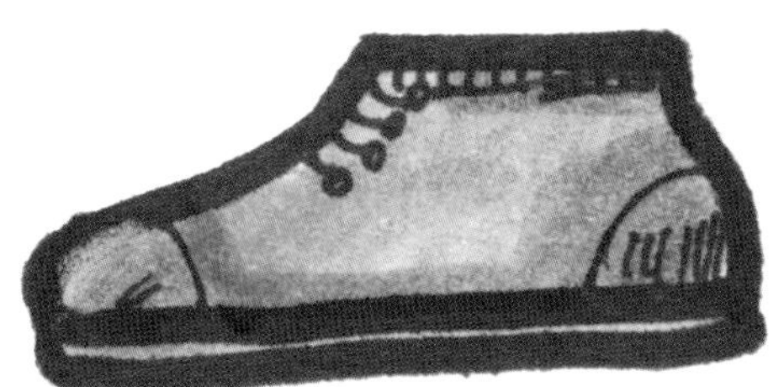

shoe **(ta) bota**
(tah) bo-tah

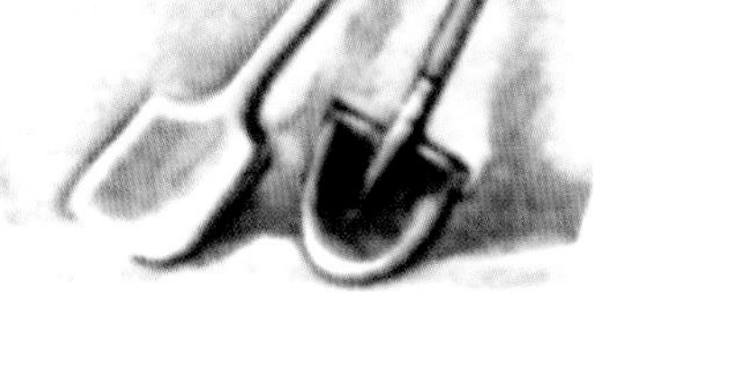

shovel **(ta) lopata**
(tah) lo-pah-tah

(to) show **ukazovat**
u-kah-zo-vaht

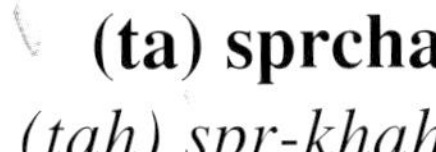

shower **(ta) sprcha**
(tah) spr-khah

shutter **(ta) okenice**
(tah) o-ke-nyi-tse

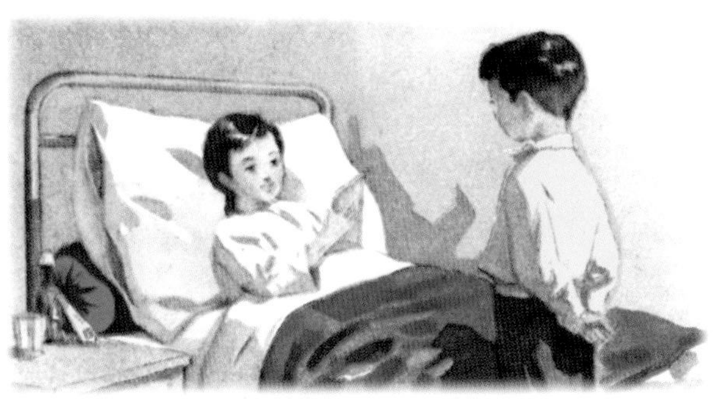

sick **nemocný**
ne-mots-nee

sieve (to) síto
(toh) see-to

(to) sing zpívat
spee-vat

(to) sit sedět
se-dyet

six šest
shest

sled (ty) sáně
(ti) saa-nye

(to) sleep spát
spaat

small **malý**
mah-leè

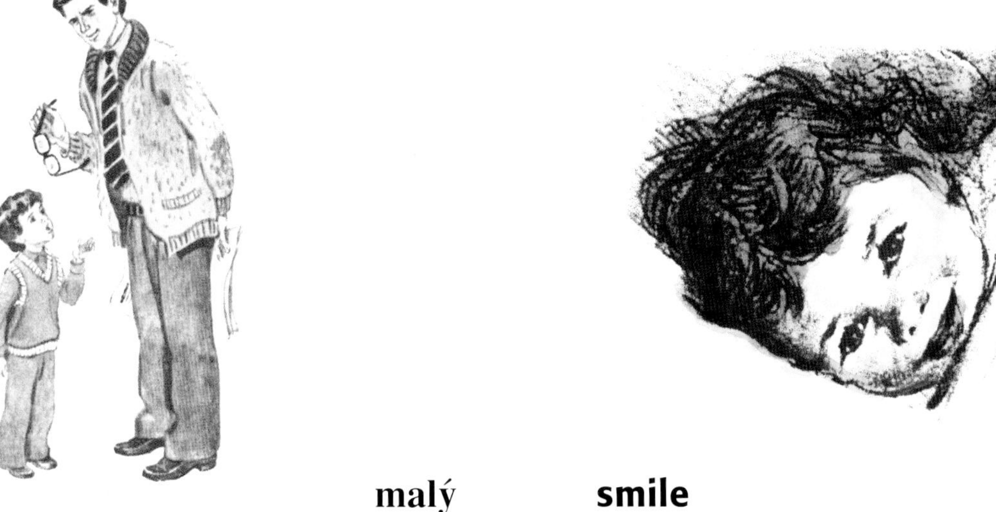

smile **usmívat se**
us-mee-vaht seh

snail **(ten) hlemýžd'**
(ten) hle-meezhd'

snake **(ten) had**
(ten) hahd

snow **(ten) sníh**
(ten) snyeeh

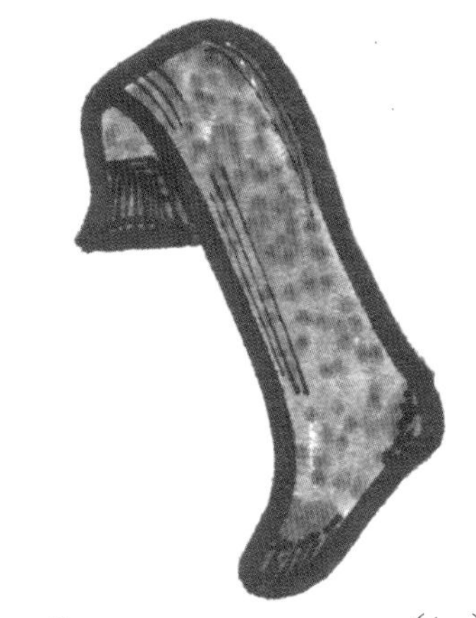

sock **(ta) ponožka**
(tah) po-nozh-kah

sofa (ta) pohovka
(tah) po-hov-kah

sparrow (ten) vrabec
(ten) vrah-bets

spider (ten) pavouk
(ten) pah-vowk

spiderweb (ta) pavučina
(tah) pah-vu-chi-nah

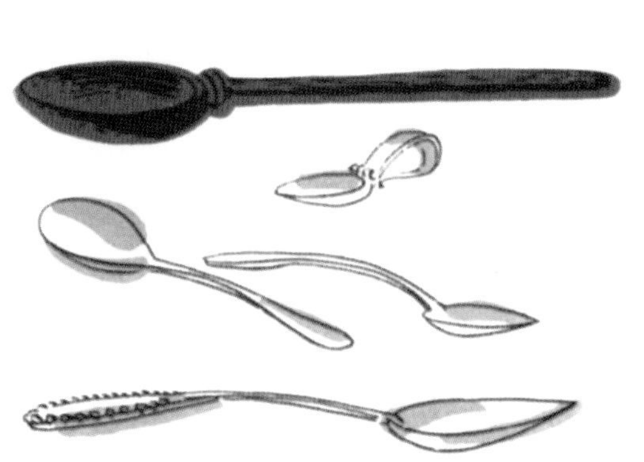

spoon (ta) lžíce
(tah) lzhee-tse

squirrel (ta) veverka
(tah) ve-ver-kah

stairs (ty) schody
(ti) skho-di

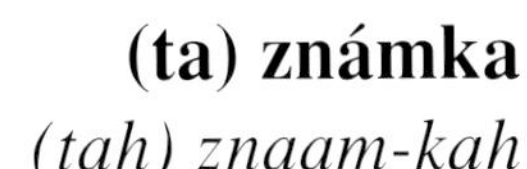

stamp (ta) známka
(tah) znaam-kah

starfish (ta) hvězdice
(tah) hvyez-dyi-tse

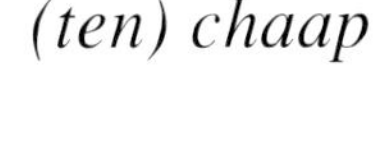

stork (ten) čáp
(ten) chaap

stove (ta) kamna
(tah) kahm-nah

strawberry (ta) jahoda
(tah) yah-ho-dah

subway **(to) metro**
(to) met-ro

sugar cube **(ta) kostka cukru**
(tah) kost-kah tsuk-ru

sun **(to) slunce**
(to) slun-tse

sunflower **(ta) slunečnice**
(tah) slu-nech-nyi-tse

sweater **(ten) svetr**
(ten) sve-tr

(to) sweep **zametat**
zah-me-taht

swing **houpat se**
how-paht se

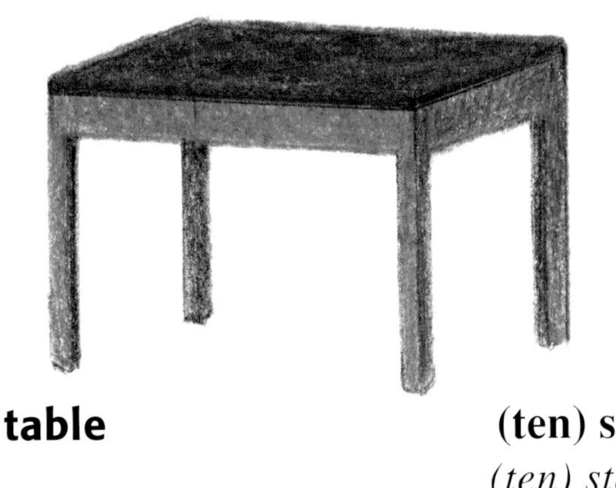

table (ten) stůl
(ten) stool

teapot (ten) čajník
(ten) chay-nyeek

teddy bear (ten) medvídek
(ten) med-vee-dek

television (ta) televize
(tah) te-le-vi-ze

10

ten deset
de-set

tent (ten) stan
(ten) stahn

theater **(to) divadlo**
(to) dyi-vahd-lo

thimble **(ten) náprstek**
(ten) naa-pr-stek

(to) think **myslit**
mi-slit

three **tři**
trzhi

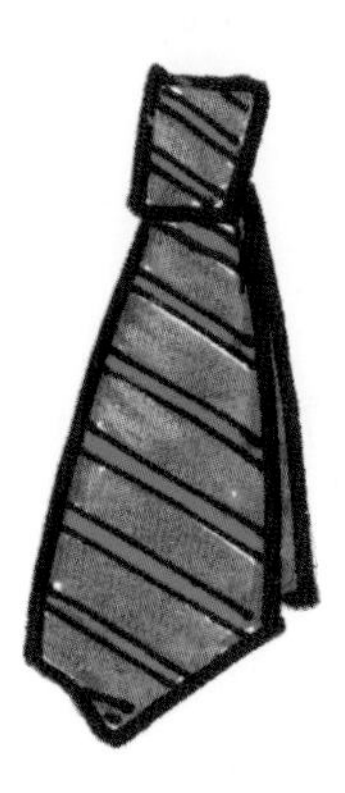

tie **(ta) kravata**
(tah) krah-vah-tah

(to) tie **uvázat**
u-vaa-zaht

tiger **(ten) tygr**
(ten) ti-gr

toaster **(ten) opékač topinek**
(ten) o-pe-kahch to-pi-nek

tomato **(to) rajče**
(toh) ray-che

toucan **(ten) tukan**
(ten) tu-kahn

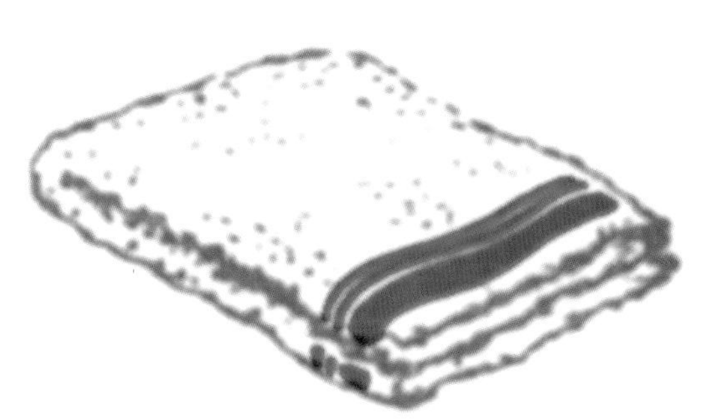

towel **(ten) ručník**
(ten) ruch-nyeek

tower **(ta) věž**
(tah) vyezh

toy box (ta) bedna na hračky
(tah) bed-nah nah hrach-ki

tracks (ta) dráha
(tah) draa-hah

train station (to) nádraží
(to) naa-drah-zhee

tray (ten) tác
(ten) taats

tree (ten) strom
(ten) strom

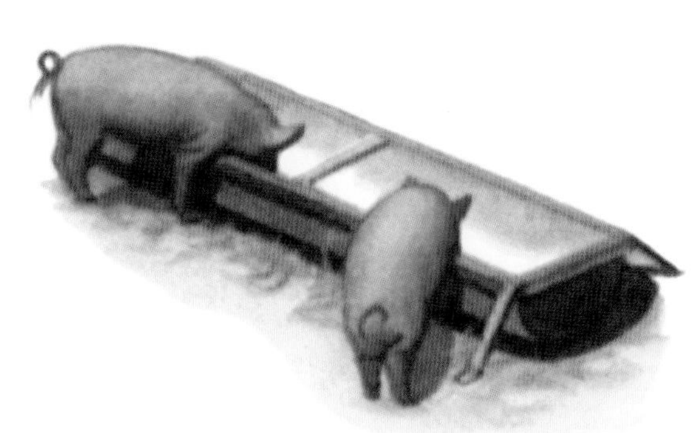

trough (to) koryto
(toh) ko-ri-to

truck **(ten) nákladní vůz**
(ten) naa-klahd-nyee vooz

trumpet **(ta) trumpeta**
(tah) trum-pe-tah

tulip **(ten) tulipán**
(ten) tu-li-paan

tunnel **(ten) tunel**
(ten) tu-nel

turtle **(ta) želva**
(tah) zhel-vah

twins **(ta) dvojčata**
(tah) dvoy-chah-tah

two **dva**
dvah

Uu

umbrella **(ten) deštník**
(ten) desh-nyeek

uphill **do kopce**
do kop-tse

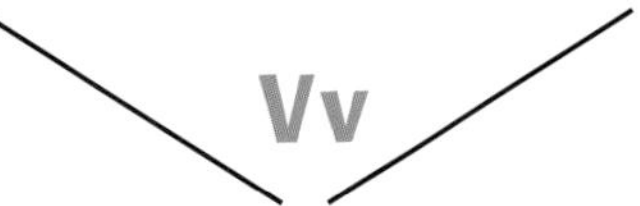

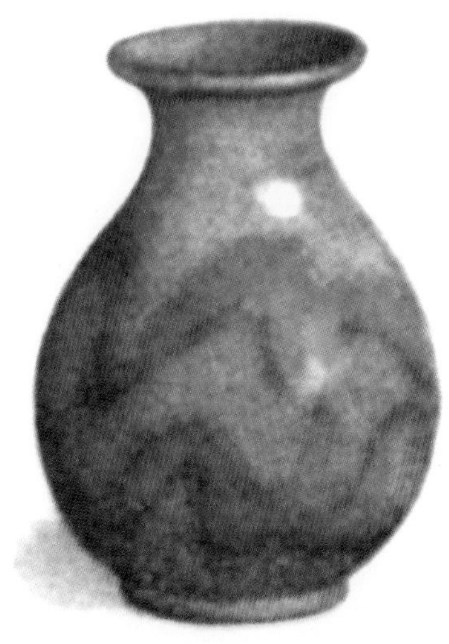

vase **(ta) váza**
(tah) vaa-zah

veil **(ten) závoj**
(ten) zaa-voy

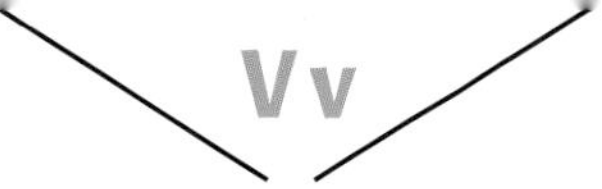

village **(ta) vesnice**
(tah) ves-nyi-tse

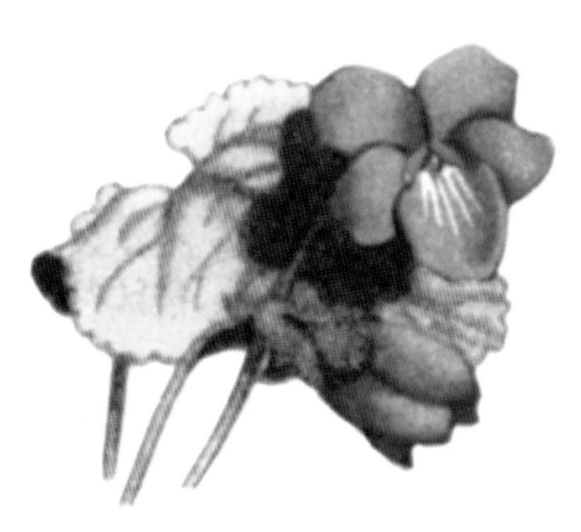

violet **(ta) fialka**
(tah) fi-yahl-kah

violin **(ty) housle**
(ti) how-sle

voyage **(ta) plavba**
(tah) plahv-bah

waiter — **(ten) číšník**
(ten) cheesh-nyeek

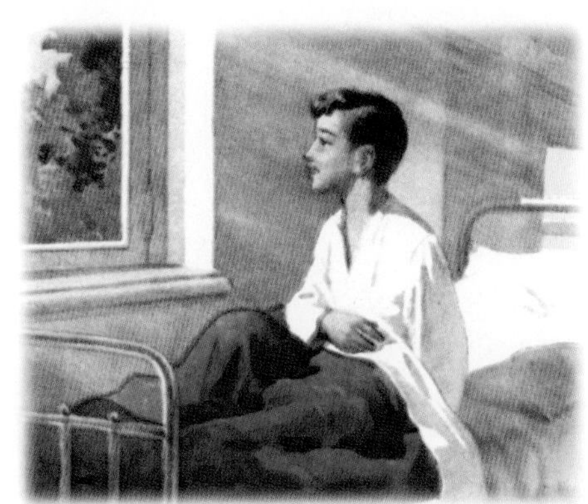

(to) wake up — **probudit se**
pro-bu-dyit se

walrus — **(ten) mrož**
(ten) mrozh

(to) wash — **mýt**
meet

watch — **(ty) hodinky**
(ti) ho-dyin-ki

(to) watch — **pozorovat**
po-zo-ro-vaht

(to) water **kropit**
kro-pit

waterfall **(ten) vodopád**
(ten) vo-do-paad

watering can **(ta) konev**
(tah) ko-nev

watermelon **(ten) meloun**
(ten) me-lown

weather vane **(ta) korouhvička**
(tah) ko-row-hvich-kah

(to) weigh **vážit**
vaa-zhit

whale **(ta) velryba**
(tah) vel-ri-bah

wheel **(to) kolo**
(to) ko-lo

wheelbarrow **(to) kolečko**
(to) ko-lech-ko

whiskers **(ty) kníry**
(ti) knyee-ri

(to) whisper **šeptat**
shep-taht

whistle **(ta) píšťalka**
(tah) pee-shtyal-kah

white **bílý**
bee-lee

wig **(ta) paruka**
(tah) pah-ru-kah

wind **(ten) vítr**
(ten) vee-tr

window **(to) okno**
(to) ok-no

wings **(ta) křídla**
(tah) krzheed-lah

winter **(ta) zima**
(tah) zi-mah

wolf **(ten) vlk**
(ten) vlk

wood **(to) dříví**
(to) drzhee-vee

word **(to) slovo**
(to) slo-vo

(to) write **psát**
psaat

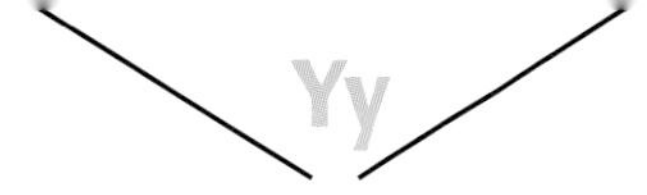

yellow

žlutý
zhlu-tee

Zz

zebra

(ta) zebra
(tah) ze-brah

Index

A

abeceda (ta) alphabet
akvárium (to) aquarium
aligátor (ten) alligator
ananas (ten) pineapple
antilopa (ta) antelope
auto (to) car

B

babička (ta) grandmother
balón (ten) balloon
banán (ten) banana
barva (ta) paint
baterka (ta) flashlight
batoh (ten) backpack
bedna na hračky (ta) toy box
beránek (ten) lamb
beruška (ta) lady bug
běžet (to) run
bílý white
bobr (ten) beaver
bota (ta) shoe
brambor (ten) potato
brána (ta) gate
bratr (ten) brother
broskev (ta) peach
brouk (ten) beetle
bruslit ice-skating
brýle (ty) glasses
buben (ten) drum

C

cesta (ta) road
cestovní pas (ten) passport
cibule (ta) onion
cirkus (ten) circus
citrón (ten) lemon
cukroví (to) candy

Č

čajník (ten) teapot
čáp (ten) stork
časopis (ten) magazine
čelenka (ta) headdress
čepice (ta) cap
černý black
červený red
číslo (to) number
číst (to) read
číšník (ten) waiter
člun (ten) boat
čmelák (ten) bumblebee
čokoláda (ta) chocolate
čtyři four

D

dalekohled (ten) binoculars
dárek (ten) present
dát (to) give
datum (to) date
dědeček (ten) grandfather
delfín (ten) dolphin
deset ten
déšť' (ten) rain
deštník (ten) umbrella
devět nine
divadlo (to) theater
dívka (ta) girl
"Dobrou Noc" "Good Night"
do kopce uphill
domeček pro panenky (ten) doll house
dort (ten) cake
dráha (ta) tracks
drak (ten) dragon
dřevorubec (ten) lumberjack
dříví (to) wood
duha (ta) rainbow
dům (ten) house
dva two
dvojčata (ta) twins
dýně (ta) pumpkin
džbán (ten) pitcher

E

Eskymák (ten) Eskimo

F

fialka (ta) violet
fontána (ta) fountain
fotoaparát (ten) camera

H

had (ten) snake
hlávkový salát (ten) lettuce
hlemýžď' (ten) snail
hnědý brown
hnízdo (to) nest
hodinky (ty) watch
holínka (ta) boot
holub (ten) pigeon
hora (ta) mountain
houba (ta) mushroom
houpačka (ta) seesaw
houpat se swing
housle (ty) violin
hraboš polní (ten) field mouse
hrad (ten) castle
hrát si (to) play
hrnec (ten) pot
hrozen vína (ten) grapes
hruška (ta) pear
hřeben (ten) comb
hudba (ta) music
husa (ta) goose
hvězdice (ta) starfish
hydrant (ten) hydrant

CH

chlapec (ten) boy
chléb (ten) bread

J

jablko (to) apple
jahoda (ta) strawberry
javorový list (ten) maple leaf
ječmen (ten) barley
jedle (ta) fir tree
jeden one
jehla (ta) needle
jelen (ten) deer
jeskyně (ta) cave
jezevec (ten) badger
ježek (ten) hedgehog
jíst (to) eat

K

kabát (ten) jacket/ coat
kabátek (ten) jacket
kabelka (ta) handbag
kachna (ta) duck
kaktus (ten) cactus
kamarád (ten) friend
kamna (ta) stove
kánoe (ta) canoe
kapesník (ten) handkerchief
kapitán (ten) captain
kapradina (ta) fern
karta (ta) card
kartáč (ten) brush
kavárna (ta) café
kbelík (ten) bucket
kejklíř (ten) juggler
klíč (ten) key
kladivo (to) hammer
klenba (ta) arch
klobouk (ten) hat
klokan (ten) kangaroo
kniha (ta) book
kníry (ty) whiskers
koberec (ten) carpet
kobylka (ta) grasshopper

kočár (ten)) coach
kočka (ta) cat
kohout (ten) rooster
kokos (ten) coconut
koláč (ten) pie
kolébka (ta) cradle
kolečko (to) wheelbarrow
kolo (to) wheel / bicycle
komín (ten) chimney
kompas (ten) compass
konev (ta) watering can
korouhvička (ta) weathervane
koruna (ta) crown
koryto (to) trough
kořen (ten) root
kosatec (ten) iris
kost (ta) bone
kostka cukru (ta) sugar cube
kostky (ty) blocks
kostky ledu (ty) ice cubes
košík (ten) basket
košile (ta) shirt
koště (to) broom
kot'átko (to) kitten
kouzelník (ten) magician
koza (ta) goat
králík (ten) rabbit
královna (ta) queen
kráva (ta) cow
kravata (ta) tie
kreslit (to) draw
krmit (to) feed
kropit (to) water
kukuřice (ta) corn
křeček (ten) hamster
křídla (ty) wings
ků∞(ten) horse
květ (ten) blossom
květina (ta) flower
kyselá okurka (ta) pickle
kytara (ta) guitar

L

láhev (ta) bottle
lampa (ta) lamp
langusta (ta) lobster
lano (to) rope
lavice (ta) bench
lední medvěd (ten) polar bear
lednička (ta) refrigerator
letadlo (to) airplane
letět (to) fly
lev (ten) lion
levandule (ta) lavender
lézt (to) crawl
lidé (ti) people
lilek (ten) eggplant
list (ten) leaf
liška (ta) fox
lít (to) pour
lízat (to) lap
lod' (ta) ship
loket (ten) elbow
lokomotiva (ta) engine
lopata (ta) shovel
lovit ryby (to) (to) fish
loupat (to) peel
lžíce (ta) spoon

M

magnet (ten) magnet
maják (ten) lighthouse
malíř (ten) painter
malina (ta) raspberry
malý small
malý papoušek (ten) love bird
mapa (ta) map
marmeláda (ta) jam
maska (ta) mask
matka (ta) mother
med (ten) honey

medvěd (ten) bear
medvídek (ten) teddy bear
medvídek koala (ten) koala bear
meloun (ten) watermelon
měsíc (ten) moon
metro (to) subway
míč (ten) ball
miminko (to) baby
mísa (ta) bowl
mlékař (ten) milkman
modrý blue
most (ten) bridge
motýl (ten) butterfly
mrak (ten) cloud
mrkev (ta) carrot
mrož (ten) walrus
mušle (ta) shell
myslit (to) think
myška (ta) mouse
mýt (to) wash
mýval (ten) raccoon

N

nábytek (ten) furniture
nádraží (to) train station
náhrdelník (ten) necklace
nahý naked
nákladní vůz (ten) truck
námořník (ten) sailor
napít se (to) drink
náprstek (ten) thimble
náramek (ten) bracelet
"Nashledanou" "Good-bye"
nástroj (ten) instrument
nést (to) carry
nemocný sick
nepořádný messy
nepromokavý plášť' (ten) raincoat
netopýr (ten) bat
noha (ta) foot / leg
nosorožec (ten) rhinoceros
noviny (ty) newspaper
nůž (ten) knife
nůžky (ty) scissors

O

obálka (ta) envelope
oběd (ten) lunch
obejmout (to) hug
oblázek (ten) pebble
obličej (ten) face
ohe∞(ten) fire
okenice (ta) shutter
okno (to) window
oko (to) eye
okurka (ta) cucumber
opékač topinek (ten) toaster
opice (ta) monkey
orel (ten) eagle
ořech (ten) nut
osel (ten) donkey
osm eight
ostrov (ten) island
otec (ten) father
otevřeno open
ovce (to) sheep
ovoce (to) fruit

P

padák (ten) parachute
palčák (ten) mitten
palma (ta) palm tree
pampeliška (ta) dandelion
panenka (ta) doll
papír (ten) paper
papoušek (ten) parrot
park (ten) park
parohy (ty) antlers
paroh (ten) antlers
paruka (ta) wig
pásek (ten) belt
pastýř (ten) shepherd
pavouk (ten) spider
pavučina (ta) spider web
pecka (ta) pit
pekař (ten) baker
pelargonie (ta) geranium

pelikán (ten) pelican
peníze (ty) money
pero (to) feather
peřina (ta) comforter
pes (ten) dog
pěst (ta) fist
pěšina (ta) path
pět five
piano (to) piano
píšťalka (ta) whistle
plakat (to) cry
plavba (ta) voyage
pláž (ta) beach
plést (to) knit
plot (ten) fence
plout (to) float / (to) sail
podkova (ta) horseshoe
podzim (ten) autumn
pohovka (ta) sofa
pohyblivé schody (ty) escalator
pole (to) field
polštář (ten) pillow
pomeranč (ten) orange
ponožka (ta) sock
pony (ten) pony
poslouchat (to) listen
postel (ta) bed
poušť' (ta) desert
pozorovat (to) watch
prám (ten) raft
prázdný empty
prase (to) pig
pravítko (to) ruler
probudit se (to) wake up
prozkoumat (to) explore

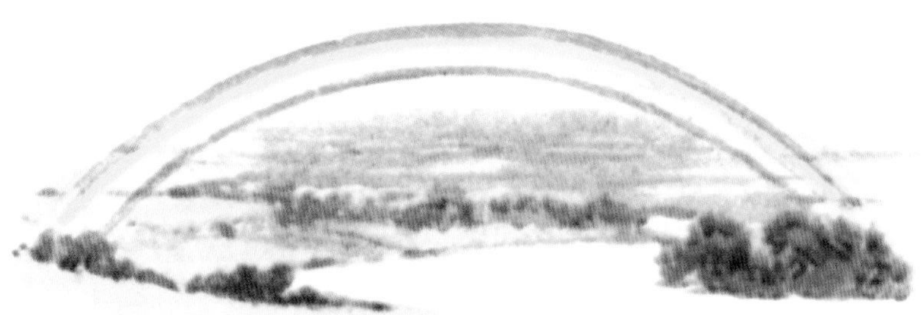

prst (ten) finger
prsten (ten) ring
přejít (to) cross
přesýpací hodiny (ty) hourglass
psát (to) write
psí bouda (ta) dog house
psací stůl (ten) desk
pštros (ten) ostrich
ptačí klec (ta) birdcage
pták (ten) bird
ptakopysk (ten) platypus
pusa (ta) mouth
pyžama (to) pajamas

R

racek (ten) seagull
rádio (to) radio
rajče (to) tomato
raketa (ta) rocket
rám (ten) frame
rohy (ty) horns
ručník (ten) towel
ruka (ta) hand
rukavice (ta) glove
růže (ta) rose
ryba (ta) fish
rys (ten) lynx
rytíř (ten) knight

Ř

ředkvička (ta) radish
řeka (ta) river

S

sáně (ty) sled
sbírat to gather
sedět (to) sit
sedm seven
seno (to) hay
sešit (ten) notebook
schody (ty) stairs
schovat se (to) hide
silnice (ta) highway
sít'ová houpačka (ta) hammock
síto (to) sieve
skládačka (ta) jigsaw puzzle
sklenice (ta) glass
skleník (ten) greeenhouse
skočit (to) jump
slavík (ten) nightingale
slepice (ta) hen
slon (ten) elephant
slovo (to) word
slunce (to) sun
slunečnice (ta) sunflower
smích (ten) laughter
snídaně (ta) breakfast
sníh (ten) snow
sosna (ta) pine
sova (ta) owl
spát (to) sleep
sprcha (ta) shower
srdce (to) heart
stan (ten) tent
starý old
strach (ten) fear
strom (ten) tree
střecha (ta) roof
stůl (ten) table
sud (ten) barrel
sůl (ta) salt
sušenka (ta) cracker
svetr (ten) sweater
svíčka (ta) candle
sýr (ten) cheese

Š

šašek (ten) clown
šátek (ten) scarf
šaty (ty) dress
šeptat (to) whisper
šeřík (ten) lilac
šest six
šíp (ten) arrow
škola (ta) school
špendlík (ten) pin
špinavý dirty
šroubovák (ten) screwdriver
štěně (to) puppy
švestka (ta) plum

T

tác (ten) tray
tahat (to) pull
talíř (ten) plate
tančit (to) dance
taxi (to) cab
televize (ta) television
tenisová raketa (ta) racket
trh (ten) marketplace
trumpeta (ta) trumpet
třešen (ta) cherry
tři three
tuč∞ák (ten) penguin
tukan (ten) toucan
tulipán (ten) tulip
tunel (ten) tunnel
tužka (ta) pencil
tygr (ten) tiger

U

ukazovat (to) show
usmívat se (to) smile
ušít (to) sew
uvázat (to) tie
uzel (ten) knot

V

Vánoční stromek (ten) Christmas tree
vařit (to) cook
váza (ta) vase
vážit (to) weigh
vážka (ta) dragonfly
včela (ta) bee
vejce (to) egg
velbloud (ten) camel
velryba (ta) whale
ventilátor (ten) fan
veslo (to) oar
veslovat (to) row
vesnice (ta) village
větev (ta) branch
veverka (ta) squirrel
věž (ta) tower
vidlička (ta) fork
visací zámek (ten) padlock
vítr (ten) wind
vlajka (ta) flag
vlk (ten) wolf
vodopád (ten) waterfall
vrabec (ten) sparrow
vůl (ten) ox
vylézt (to) climb
vývěska (ta) bulletin board

Z

záclona (ta) curtain
zahrada (ta) garden
zámek (ten) lock
zametat (to) sweep
zaoceánská loď (ta) ocean liner
záplata (ta) patch
zátka (ta) cork
zavazadla (ty) luggage
zavírací špendlík (ten) safety pin
závoj (ten) veil
zebra (ta) zebra
zelený green
zelí (to) cabbage
zeměkoule (ta) globe
zima (ta) winter
zlatá rybka (ta) goldfish
zmrzlina (ta) ice cream
známka (ta) stamp
zobat (to) peck
zpívat (to) sing
zrcadlo (to) mirror
zvon (ten) bell
zvonit (to) ring

Ž

žába (ta) frog
žací stroj na trávu (ten) lawn mower
žárovka (ta) lightbulb
žebřík (ten) ladder
žehlička (ta) iron
želva (ta) turtle
židle (ta) chair
žirafa (ta) giraffe
žlutý yellow
žně (ty) harvest
žokej (ten) jockey
žralok (ten) shark

Folk Tales from Bohemia
Adolf Wenig
This folk tale collection is one of a kind, focusing uniquely on humankind's struggle with evil in the world. Delicately ornate red and black text and illustrations set the mood.
Ages 9 and up
90 pages • red and black illustrations • 5 1/2 x 8 1/4 • 0-7818-0718-2 • W • $14.95hc • (786)

Czech, Moravian and Slovak Fairy Tales
Parker Fillmore
Fifteen different classic, regional folk tales and 23 charming illustrations whisk the reader to places of romance, deception, royalty, and magic.
Ages 12 and up
243 pages • 23 b/w illustrations • 5 1/2 x 8 1/4 • 0-7818-0714-X • W • $14.95 hc • (792)

Glass Mountain: Twenty-Eight Ancient Polish Folk Tales and Fables
W.S. Kuniczak
Illustrated by Pat Bargielski
As a child in a far-away misty corner of Volhynia, W.S. Kuniczak was carried away to an extraordinary world of magic and illusion by the folk tales of his Polish nurse.
171 pages • 6 x 9 • 8 illustrations • 0-7818-0552-X • W • $16.95hc • (645)

Old Polish Legends
Retold by F.C. Anstruther
Wood engravings by J. Sekalski
This fine collection of eleven fairy tales, with an introduction by Zymunt Nowakowski, was first published in Scotland during World War II.
66 pages • 7 1/4 x 9 • 11 woodcut engravings • 0-7818-0521-X • W • $11.95hc • (653)

Folk Tales from Russia
by Donald A. Mackenzie
With nearly 200 pages and 8 full-page black-and-white illustrations, the reader will be charmed by these legendary folk tales that symbolically weave magical fantasy with the historic events of Russia's past.
Ages 12 and up
192 pages • 8 b/w illustrations • 5 1/2 x 8 1/4 • 0-7818-0696-8 • W • $12.50hc • (788)

Fairy Gold: A Book of Classic English Fairy Tales
Chosen by Ernest Rhys
Illustrated by Herbert Cole
Forty-nine imaginative black and white illustrations accompany thirty classic tales, including such beloved stories as "Jack and the Bean Stalk" and "The Three Bears."
Ages 12 and up
236 pages • 5 1/2 x 8 1/4 • 49 b/w illustrations • 0-7818-0700-X • W • $14.95hc • (790)

Tales of Languedoc: From the South of France
Samuel Jacques Brun
For readers of all ages, here is a masterful collection of folk tales from the south of France.
Ages 12 and up
248 pages • 33 b/w sketches • 5 1/2 x 8 1/4 • 0-7818-0715-8 • W • $14.95hc • (793)

Twenty Scottish Tales and Legends
Edited by Cyril Swinson
Illustrated by Allan Stewart
Twenty enchanting stories take the reader to an extraordinary world of magic harps, angry giants, mysterious spells and gallant Knights.
Ages 9 and up
215 pages • 5 1/2 x 8 1/4 • 8 b/w illustrations • 0-7818-0701-8 • W • $14.95 hc • (789)

Swedish Fairy Tales
Translated by H. L. Braekstad
A unique blending of enchantment, adventure, comedy, and romance make this collection of Swedish fairy tales a must-have for any library.
Ages 9 and up
190 pages • 21 b/w illustrations • 51/2 x 81/4 • 0-7818-0717-4 • W • $12.50hc • (787)

The Little Mermaid and Other Tales
Hans Christian Andersen
Here is a near replica of the first American edition of 27 classic fairy tales from the masterful Hans Christian Andersen.
Ages 9 and up
508 pages • b/w illustrations • 6 x 9 • 0-7818-0720-4 • W • $19.95hc • (791)

Pakistani Folk Tales: Toontoony Pie and Other Stories
Ashraf Siddiqui and Marilyn Lerch
Illustrated by Jan Fairservis
In these 22 folk tales are found not only the familiar figures of folklore—kings and beautiful princesses—but the magic of the Far East, cunning jackals, and wise holy men.
Ages 7 and up
158 pages • 6 1/2 x 8 1/2 • 38 illustrations • 0-7818-0703-4 • W • $12.50hc • (784)

Folk Tales from Chile
Brenda Hughes
This selection of 15 tales gives a taste of the variety of Chile's rich folklore. Fifteen charming illustrations accompany the text.
Ages 7 and up
121 pages • 5 1/2 x 8 1/4 • 15 illustrations • 0-7818-0712-3 • W • $12.50hc • (785)